694
WA

Walker, Lester

Carpentry for
children

DATE			
NO 06 '85	NO 6 '90	AP 27 '02	
DE 17 85	JY 9 '92	OC 25 '04	
JA 21 '86	AG 4 '92	MR 22 '06	
MR 5 '86	SE 4 '92		
MR 21 '86	MR 20 '93		
MR 5 '87	JE 24 '93		
MR 23 '87	AG 6 '93		
MR 30 '88	MAY 03 '95		
AG 22 '89	MAY 17 '96		
OC 3 '89	JAN 20 '97		
JE 19 '90	JA 30 '98		

© THE BAKER & TAYLOR CO.

Carpentry for Children

Carpentry for Children

LESTER WALKER

PREFACE BY DAVID MACAULAY

THE OVERLOOK PRESS
WOODSTOCK, NEW YORK

First published in 1982 by
The Overlook Press
Lewis Hollow Road
Woodstock, N.Y. 12498

Library of Congress Cataloging in Publication Data

Walker, Lester
Carpentry for Children.

Summary: A step-by-step guide to carrying out
childrens' carpentry projects such as a birdhouse, candle
chandelier, doll cradle, puppet theater, and coaster car.

1. Carpentry—Juvenile literature. [1. Carpentry. 2.
Handicraft] I. Title.

TH5607.W34   694   82-3469
ISBN 0-87951-155-9   AACR2

Printed in the USA

To my son, Jess

Table of Contents

Using Your Tools

Building Your Workshop

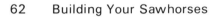

One-Day Projects

Weekend Projects

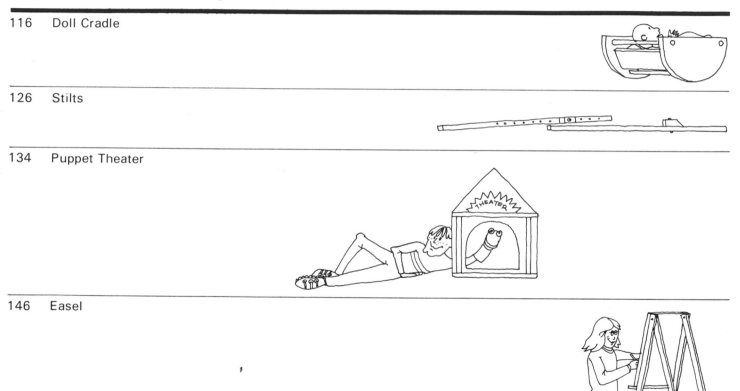

One-Week Projects

Preface

I have been making things all my life, from working cardboard elevators with paper accordian doors to small buildings out of wood scraps. With increasing family affluence, I moved on to plastic aircraft carriers, the twenty-mule team, and, ultimately, a forty watt amplifier — which, to my absolute amazement, worked.

For almost as long as I've been making things, I've been reading instructions for making things. When I was ten, I was given a copy of the 1895 "Boy's Own Paper" annual. It contained instructions for building the "Boy's Own Windmill", the "Boy's Own Simple Camera", and the "Boy's Own Racing Catamaran." Although I hadn't the slightest idea what a catamaran was, not to mention a racing one, I remember poring over those instructions with great satisfaction. In my imagination I built them all and they all worked perfectly and they all looked at least as good as the drawings in the book.

Oh the joy of a challenge, of good, well-illustrated instructions and an imagination.

Ten years later, while studying architecture, I discovered that what I had unsuspectingly thought of as fun was in fact called *The Design Process*. With the convenience of a name for my activities came the reassurance that a lot of other people had been innocently having fun and that they, too, didn't want to stop.

Although Lester Walker and I have never met and in fact have communicated only through letters, I am sure that we both indulge in a similar kind of fun. We both need to know how things are made and we both believe that this underrated pleasure should be encouraged and shared. The only significant difference between our books is that I write mostly in the past tense and Lester writes mostly in the present. Tenses aside and audiences up front, we are both, I believe, writing for the future. That fact alone makes writing this preface a pleasure. But the obvious good time that the four young carpenters seem to be having throughout the book makes the opportunity irresistable.

Carpentry for Children combines two of life's greatest pleasures. First, it describes clearly and logically how a variety of objects can be made. Second, it shows someone else doing all the work. All we have to do is turn the pages. What could be more satisfying? Just seeing and understanding how a workbench or a raft or a coaster car is made is a very rewarding experience. The instructions are very clear and economical, the drawings are simple, accurate, and amusing and the photographs prove that the instructions and drawings work. The combination of all three makes us a part of problem, process and product without a single cut or a sneaker full of sawdust.

So what could be more satisfying than simply reading this book? The answer is obvious — using it. What makes *Carpentry for Children* (of all ages) important is its ability to explain how things are made and to encourage us to want to make them. The innate enthusiasm captured on each page becomes an irresistable welcome to the world of cuts and sawdust.

But there are other things that make *Carpentry for Children* important. Even if you don't happen to need a puppet theater or a tugboat, there will be something in the collection of projects to tickle your fancy and get you started. And getting started is what the book is all about. Its ultimate purpose is not, it seems to me, to fill the reader's house with wooden objects, but to fill the reader's mind with a sense of order and process and an appreciation of craft. While the projects encourage and build confidence, they also impart an awareness of materials, an appreciation for and knowledge of tools, along with the development of certain basic skills. They introduce the concept of patience, which — at least early on — is invariably locked in mortal combat with enthusiasm. All these ingredients combine to create the possibility of craftsmanship. And when craftsmanship and imagination are combined the real fun begins.

Just as my preface is a starting point for this book, so *Carpentry for Children* is a preface to countless unwritten chapters in the lives of its readers. Its message and enthusiasm will continue to influence those lives long after the raft has sunk — or at least has been converted into a racing catamaran.

David Macaulay
Providence, Rhode Island

Introduction

It's often difficult to describe why one takes the time to write or illustrate a book. This book, *Carpentry for Children*, presented no such problem. It was most definitely inspired by three children:

The first is Jason Conforti of Klamath Falls, Oregon, who wrote me a very encouraging letter with the help of Elaine Reed-Ehm, the children's librarian of the Klamath County Library. Jason had read my first book, *Housebuilding for Children*, and suggested that I write a book that illustrated how children could build coaster cars, just as *Housebuilding for Children* taught children how to build houses. Ms. Reed-Ehm supported Jason's idea and convinced me that there were few, if any, books that taught carpentry, especially the building of coaster cars, to children. I found their ideas interesting, and, of course, I'm delighted that they took time to write. Now, almost four years after receiving their letters, the result is this book.

The second child is my son, Jess, who, from the time when he was five or six years old, has been interested in carpentry and woodworking projects. When he was eight years old, we had so much fun working together, with nine of his friends, on *Housebuilding for Children*, that we felt it would be even more fun if we did it again with smaller projects and a few different friends. I felt that this would be my last chance to work with him as a child, so, four years later, we enthusiastically went ahead with the book. He chose the friends and projects, and I made arrangements with parents, got the materials, designed the projects, and set up the photography. And off we went! Needless to say, we had great fun, as all the smiling faces in the photographs throughout the book show.

The third child is me. When I was ten years old, living in Pittsburgh, Pennsylvania, I was always tinkering with wood or any other material I could find to make projects ranging in scale from a small boat to a large, shacklike shelter. The photograph on the next page is personally quite nostalgic because it shows me with my best childhood friends in our coaster cars (we called them dinks), made from various pieces of junk. For example, with some help from my grandfather, I made my car from a wastebasket, a wood frame, three different wagon wheels, and some rope. The photograph was taken on the day of a big race that my friends and I had arranged. It had all the elements of an Indianapolis 500 event: prizes, newspaper coverage, a judges' stand with a finish line, and, of course, a wild cheering crowd. We were so proud of our coaster cars.

With my own childhood experiences providing firsthand knowledge, with Jess and his friends anxious to build, and with the inspiring letter from Jason Conforti, I felt I could provide a valuable service to the coaster car-lovers, the would-be carpenter-children of the world, by offering them a book with plans and pictures showing children teaching themselves carpentry by building projects that they loved.

Special thanks to: the carpentry crew for their hard work and patience; the parents of the children for their understanding; Gail Cadden, a wonderful Woodstock, New York graphic designer, for her help in developing the cartoon characters; Kevin Hyde, who did such beautiful work with the printing of the photographs; Sunfrost Farms of Woodstock for the orange crates; Donna and Nickie Pelham for their help with the props; and Elisabeth Mashinic for her work with the text.

The author (far left), photographed when he was ten years old, with his friends and their coaster cars on the day of a big race.

Meeting the Carpenters

Four terrific kids made up the hardworking carpentry crew who built the projects and posed for the pictures shown in this book. We worked all day Tuesdays and Thursdays during the summer and on weekends once school started. It took us three-and-one-half months to complete and photograph all the work.

Reading through the book, you'll see that some of the projects are designed for the seven-to-eleven age group — the block set, the tugboat, and the lemonade stand — and some are designed for the eleven-to-fourteen age group — the raft, stilts, and the coaster car. The book is written so that any child who can read should be able to build any of the projects with or without adult supervision. Children from the ages of seven to fourteen should find many projects that are of interest. Naturally, Molly, Adam, Jess, and Ben each had his or her favorite projects, which were arrived at through extensive use and testing. Molly liked the lemonade stand, Adam the coaster car, Jess the raft, and Ben the stilts. But if they had been carpenters four years ago, they may have liked the doll cradle, the tugboat, or the puppet theater. The point is that there is a project for everybody, and everybody can become a carpenter with hard work and patience. Molly, Adam, Jess, and Ben are to be congratulated for working so hard, and they will benefit, having developed their natural skills by learning the carpentry craft. How about you?

HURRY UP, GUYS. THEY'RE SHOWING OUR PICTURES!

Jess Walker, 12. Molly Holm, 10. Ben Holm, 13. Adam Levitt, 11.

Using This Book

This book is arranged as a chronological, step-by-step guide to learning carpentry. If you follow each direction as it first appears, from buying and learning how to use your tools to building your workshop and the projects, you'll have very little trouble in learning the carpentry craft.

Reading the book, note that you'll receive a direction on the even-numbered pages. Usually, there will be a photograph or photographs of the same direction being performed on the facing page by Molly, Ben, Jess, and Adam. Study the photographs and compare them with the directions until you understand what you are supposed to do. The photographs are meant to help you understand the directions.

In order to build each project, you'll have to perform a certain amount of tasks (steps). It's important not to go to step two until step one is completed and done well. You'll often find that once you get started on a project, it's so much fun that you lose patience because you desire to see the finished product. But the real test — the real craft of carpentry — is just this: you must be patient, you must be careful, and you must work slowly but surely to make a project of which you can be proud.

Before beginning, you should read this book cover to cover at least twice to fully understand the projects, the sequencing of the tasks, and the skills you'll need to learn how to become a carpenter.

Molly, Jess, Adam, and Ben studying Carpentry for Children.

Buying Your Tools

It's very important to buy tools that you can handle. If they're too heavy, too large, or not sharp enough, you'll find that you'll have to do a lot of tiring extra work. If they're the right size and weight, however, and they work well, they'll make your carpentry work fun. Below is a list of tools needed to learn carpentry and make the projects that are illustrated later in this book. Your parents or teacher may want to buy these tools for your use, or they may want to let you use theirs, but it's best to get your own set and have responsibility for it.

The crosscut saw is the most critical tool. It must be sharp and have a blade that does not exceed 14". Several companies make what is called a "tool box saw," the perfect size. Every other tool can be standard adult size with the exception of the hammer, which should weigh under 12 oz.

Hammer	Under 12 oz. in weight	
Crosscut saw	12" to 14" maximum blade length	
Keyhole saw	10" blade	
Brace and Bit	Buy an "open ratchet bit brace" and a 1" and a ⅜" auger bit	
Square	Buy the most inexpensive — usually one with a plastic handle	
Measuring tape	8' long tape with a belt clip	
Adjustable wrench	8" long	
Screwdriver	10" long	
Pliers	6" long	
Sandpaper	See instructions for each project	
Paint brush	See instructions for each project	
Bandages	One small box for cuts	
Carpenter's apron	Try to get one free at your local lumberyard	

The group visiting the hardware store and learning about tools and how to buy them.

Buying Your Materials

There is a list of all the materials you'll need at the beginning of each project, including the building of your workshop. Take a pad and pencil and write all these materials down so that when you call or visit your lumberyard you'll make no mistakes. Be at home when the materials are delivered so you can pay for them and have them unloaded in a safe place.

Below is a chart showing the nail sizes and types that you'll be using. Refer to it when ordering your materials.

really 1½"x3½". The reason is that when the 2x4 is dried (usually in a factory), it shrinks to a 1½"x3½" size. This difference has been accounted for in all the projects in this book.

If you don't fully understand the sizes of nails and lumber, talk to someone at your lumberyard. Get him or her to show you some of these materials and explain them to you. All good carpenters hang out at the lumberyard!

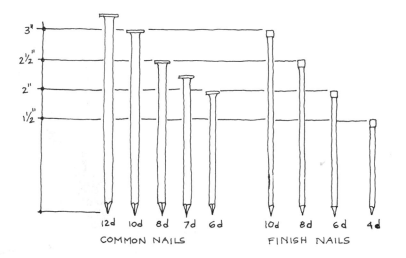

The common nail has a heavy cross-section and is designed for rough work such as nailing 2x4s together. The thinner finishing nail is used for finished carpentry work, such as nailing ¾"-thick boards together.

The nail size-unit is called a "penny" and is abbreviated with the lower-case letter d. It indicates the length of the nail. A 12d (twelve penny) nail is 3¼" long. It decreases ¼" for each penny.

When ordering lumber, don't be alarmed that it's ½" smaller than what it's called. For example, a 2x4 is

The group visiting the lumberyard and learning about lumber and how to buy it.

Getting Help

As you work your way through this book, building some of your favorite projects, there will be times when you'll need help. Perhaps you'll be having trouble using a particular tool or understanding some of the plans. But whatever the problem, don't hesitate to ask your parents, teacher, or someone who'll be happy to help you.

As mentioned before, it's best to read this book cover to cover a few times to fully understand what you must do to teach yourself the art of carpentry. As you read, pay particular attention to the section devoted to using tools. Then, after you've assembled your tools, ask a parent or teacher to watch you practice until you feel comfortable with the tools. Be very careful with the saw — the source of cuts — and the hammer — the source of bruises. If there are any questions about the use of a tool, reread the "Using Your Tools" chapter or ask a good local carpenter for help. The hardware store or lumberyard where you bought the tools will, also, often be of great help.

Get criticism from your parents, teacher, and friends about the quality of your work as you practice with your tools. Can you saw better or hit the nail straighter? Ask how your work can be improved.

Carefully review the tasks you'll have to perform to build the projects you've chosen. Keep asking questions until you fully understand. And, of course, working with friends can be the most fun and the best source of help.

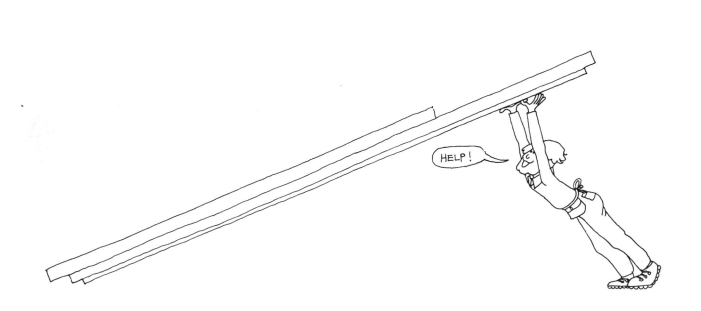

HELP!

The carpenters learning the dangers of the hammer and saw.

Using Your Tools

This chapter is written and illustrated to teach you how to use the basic hand tools of carpentry. Take these pages, along with your tools and some scraps of soft wood, and practice using your tools as shown in the accompanying directions. Drive and pull one-hundred or more nails with the hammer until you can do it well. Saw one-hundred or more cuts until you can do it perfectly straight. Keep working and learning the tools until you feel confident.

When you feel comfortable with each tool, go on to the next chapter and build your workshop. As you build, take time out to practice, as shown in the photograph on the facing page. Remember, you're teaching yourself to be a good carpenter.

Molly practicing drilling, Ben practicing hammering, and Jess and Adam using the saw.

The Hammer

Below are the three jobs that you'll be performing with your hammer. To hammer a nail into wood, it's important to tap it a few times to give it a start so it'll be straight and you don't have to hold it. Then you can hit the nail harder, and if you miss, you won't get hurt. Remember, it isn't important how many times you hit the nail to drive it all the way into the wood. It *is* important how straight it goes. Take your time, and swing the hammer accurately.

1 NAILING

GRAB THE HAMMER NEAR THE MIDDLE OF THE HANDLE AND TURN YOUR WRIST TO DRIVE IN THE NAIL.

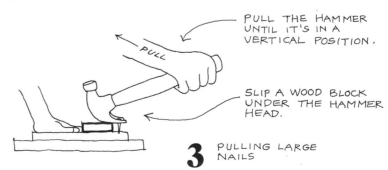

STEADY THE NAIL WITH YOUR OTHER HAND.

HOLD THE WORK STEADY WITH YOUR OTHER HAND.

PULL THE HAMMER UNTIL IT'S IN A VERTICAL POSITION.

PULL

SLIP THE CLAW OF THE HAMMER UNDER THE NAIL HEAD.

2 PULLING SMALL NAILS

PULL THE HAMMER UNTIL IT'S IN A VERTICAL POSITION.

PULL

SLIP A WOOD BLOCK UNDER THE HAMMER HEAD.

3 PULLING LARGE NAILS

Adam practicing with the hammer.

The Crosscut Saw

After you've drawn a pencil line showing where you want to saw, you're ready to start. Grasp the handle of the saw firmly in your dominant hand and draw or pull the saw up several times, with the thumb of your other hand guiding the blade on the wood where the saw cut is to be made. Doing this will make a small groove in the wood that will keep the saw blade in place so you can begin to saw along the pencil line. When you've reached the end of the cut, take short sawing strokes and hold the waste piece so that it doesn't break off and splinter. The saw is your most dangerous tool. Begin slowly and practice as much as you can.

1 PULL THE SAW TOWARD YOU THREE OR FOUR TIMES UNTIL YOU GET A GROOVE STARTED.

45°

PULL

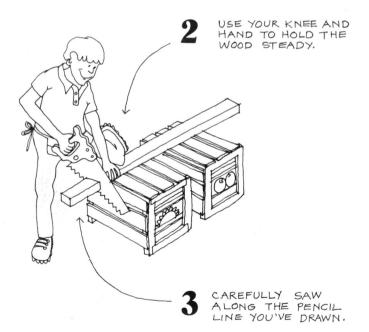

2 USE YOUR KNEE AND HAND TO HOLD THE WOOD STEADY.

3 CAREFULLY SAW ALONG THE PENCIL LINE YOU'VE DRAWN.

Adam and Ben practicing the crosscut saw.

29

The Keyhole Saw

The keyhole saw is used primarily to cut out curved shapes. First a hole is drilled, then the thin keyhole saw is inserted into the hole to begin the sawing. This tool works best when it's kept in an upright position, perpendicular with your work, as shown in the drawing below. Cut along your pencil line carefully, using long, easy strokes.

3 USE THE VISE TO HOLD SMALL PIECES OF WOOD WHILE YOU SAW THEM.

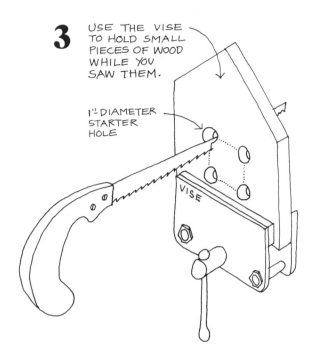

1" DIAMETER STARTER HOLE

VISE

USE YOUR KNEE AND LEFT HAND TO HOLD THE WOOD STEADY.

1 A HOLE IS DRILLED WITH THE 1" DRILL BIT TO MAKE A STARTING PLACE FOR THE KEYHOLE SAW.

2 SAW ALONG YOUR PENCIL LINE, KEEPING THE SAW IN A STRAIGHT UP-AND-DOWN POSITION.

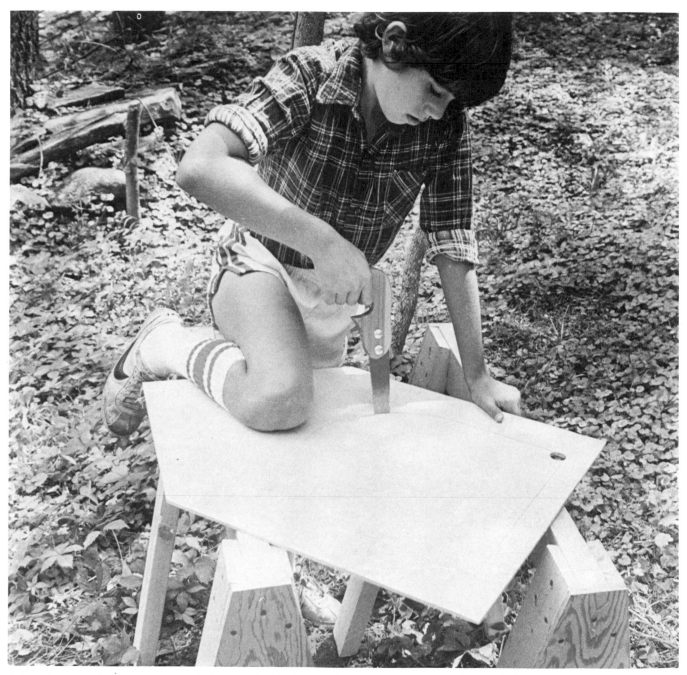

Adam inserts the keyhole saw into a drilled hole and begins to cut out a piece of plywood.

The Brace and Bit

Below are the five steps taken to drill a perfect hole with your brace and bit. Step five is particularly important because it shows you how to drill without breaking through the wood at the bottom of the hole, which leaves a ragged, splintered edge. Also, you may have trouble drilling a straight hole. This problem can be easily solved by asking a friend to stand back and line you up as you drill.

2 PLACE THE DRILL BIT INTO THE JAWS AND TURN THE HANDLE CLOCKWISE UNTIL THE JAWS FIRMLY GRAB IT.

JAWS →

1 TURN THE HANDLE COUNTERCLOCKWISE UNTIL THE JAWS ARE OPEN.

4 TURN THE HANDLE CLOCKWISE TO DRILL THE HOLE.

3 HOLD THE HEAD OF THE DRILL AGAINST YOUR STOMACH AND PRESS FORWARD.

5 TO GET A PERFECT HOLE, DRILL THROUGH THE WOOD UNTIL THE POINT OF THE DRILL IS SHOWING ON THE OTHER SIDE, THEN REMOVE THE BIT FROM THE HOLE, TURN THE PIECE OVER, AND DRILL FROM THE OTHER SIDE, USING THE LITTLE HOLE TO START THE BIT AGAIN.

Molly practicing with the brace and bit.

The Square

The square, sometimes called the "try square," is used to draw straight, perpendicular lines for sawing. When you use the square, press the handle hard against the edge of the wood, then draw a pencil line along the steel edge, perpendicular to the edge of the wood. You're now ready to make a perfect saw cut.

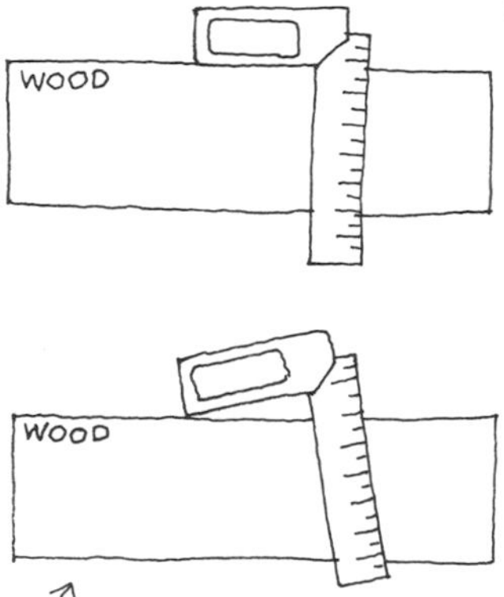

1 PRESS THE HANDLE OF THE SQUARE HARD AGAINST THE EDGE OF THE WOOD.

WOOD

WOOD

THIS IS A COMMON MISTAKE. THERE'S NOT ENOUGH PRESSURE ON THE HANDLE.

3 DRAW A PENCIL LINE ALONG THE EDGE OF THE SQUARE'S STEEL BLADE.

2 KEEP PRESSING THE HANDLE AGAINST THE EDGE OF THE WOOD WITH YOUR OTHER HAND.

Adam using the square to make a straight, perpendicular line.

The Tape

The 8'-long measuring tape is a marked coil of steel tape that unrolls to measure boards up to 8' long. You can use the tape by yourself by catching the hook on the edge of the board and pulling the cover away from that edge. Or, have a friend help you by holding one end of the tape. Measure the feet first, then the inches, and then the parts of inches. For example, if you must measure 1'-6½" (' is the symbol for feet and " is the symbol for inches), first find the 1' mark, then move along the tape until you find the 6" mark, then move farther along to the first ½" mark.

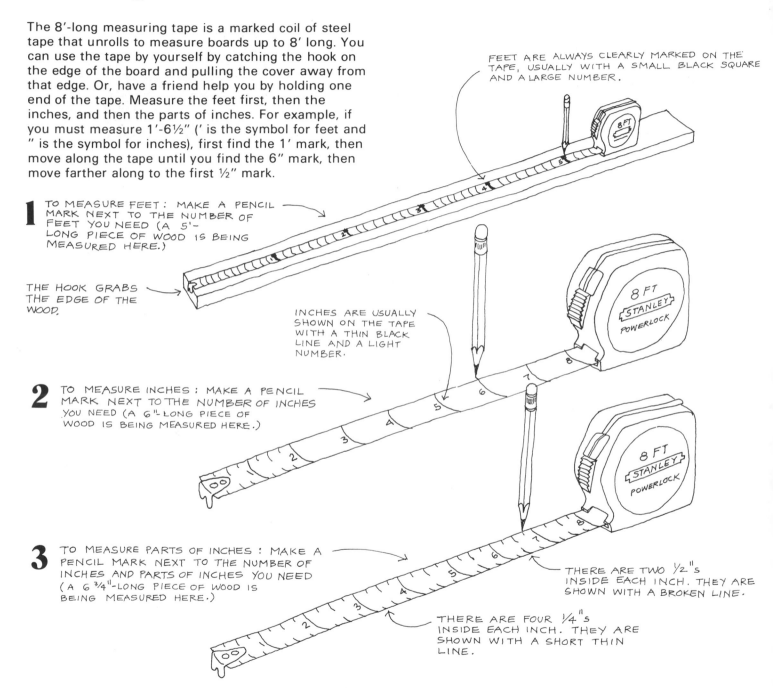

FEET ARE ALWAYS CLEARLY MARKED ON THE TAPE, USUALLY WITH A SMALL BLACK SQUARE AND A LARGE NUMBER.

1 TO MEASURE FEET: MAKE A PENCIL MARK NEXT TO THE NUMBER OF FEET YOU NEED (A 5'-LONG PIECE OF WOOD IS BEING MEASURED HERE.)

THE HOOK GRABS THE EDGE OF THE WOOD.

INCHES ARE USUALLY SHOWN ON THE TAPE WITH A THIN BLACK LINE AND A LIGHT NUMBER.

2 TO MEASURE INCHES: MAKE A PENCIL MARK NEXT TO THE NUMBER OF INCHES YOU NEED (A 6"-LONG PIECE OF WOOD IS BEING MEASURED HERE.)

3 TO MEASURE PARTS OF INCHES: MAKE A PENCIL MARK NEXT TO THE NUMBER OF INCHES AND PARTS OF INCHES YOU NEED (A 6¾"-LONG PIECE OF WOOD IS BEING MEASURED HERE.)

THERE ARE TWO ½"s INSIDE EACH INCH. THEY ARE SHOWN WITH A BROKEN LINE.

THERE ARE FOUR ¼"s INSIDE EACH INCH. THEY ARE SHOWN WITH A SHORT THIN LINE.

Molly using the tape to measure a board.

The Adjustable Wrench, Screwdriver, and Pliers

The adjustable wrench, screwdriver, and pliers are three of the easiest tools to use. Simply place the tool around or in the slot of the screwhead, grab the handle of each, and turn in a clockwise direction to tighten the screw or in a counterclockwise direction to loosen the screw.

The adjustable wrench gets its name from its ability to adjust its jaws to grab a screwhead (usually hexagonal in shape). The screwdriver fits into the slot of a round-headed screw, and you must squeeze the handles of the pliers to grab the screwhead.

Often you'll need to use most of your strength to use these three tools.

3 KEEP TURNING THE WRENCH HANDLE UNTIL THE SCREW IS TIGHT.

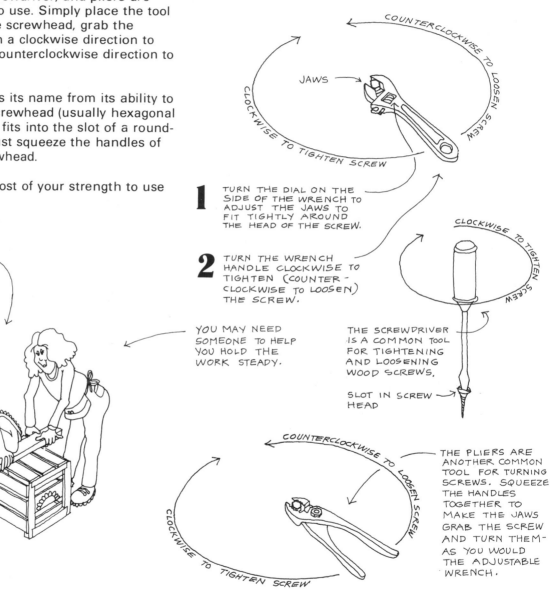

COUNTERCLOCKWISE TO LOOSEN SCREW

CLOCKWISE TO TIGHTEN SCREW

JAWS

1 TURN THE DIAL ON THE SIDE OF THE WRENCH TO ADJUST THE JAWS TO FIT TIGHTLY AROUND THE HEAD OF THE SCREW.

2 TURN THE WRENCH HANDLE CLOCKWISE TO TIGHTEN (COUNTER-CLOCKWISE TO LOOSEN) THE SCREW.

YOU MAY NEED SOMEONE TO HELP YOU HOLD THE WORK STEADY.

CLOCKWISE TO TIGHTEN SCREW

THE SCREWDRIVER IS A COMMON TOOL FOR TIGHTENING AND LOOSENING WOOD SCREWS.

SLOT IN SCREW HEAD

COUNTERCLOCKWISE TO LOOSEN SCREW

CLOCKWISE TO TIGHTEN SCREW

THE PLIERS ARE ANOTHER COMMON TOOL FOR TURNING SCREWS. SQUEEZE THE HANDLES TOGETHER TO MAKE THE JAWS GRAB THE SCREW AND TURN THEM - AS YOU WOULD THE ADJUSTABLE WRENCH.

Ben using the adjustable wrench to tighten a hex-head screw.

Painting

Painting is the most fun of carpentry work because you can change a rough-looking project into a finished object very quickly. Below are the three steps needed to do a professional paint job. If you follow them and have patience, your painted projects will look beautiful.

The primer paint mentioned in step two is a white, quick-drying enamel or alcohol-based paint. It clogs the pores of the wood and, after it dries, provides a hard, white, sandable surface upon which the final, finish coat of enamel paint (step three) will shine.

Take care of your brushes by cleaning them with rags and turpentine, and store them for future use in a glass of turpentine. Clean your hands with turpentine on a rag, then wash with soap and water. Be sure to store your paints with the lids tightly sealed.

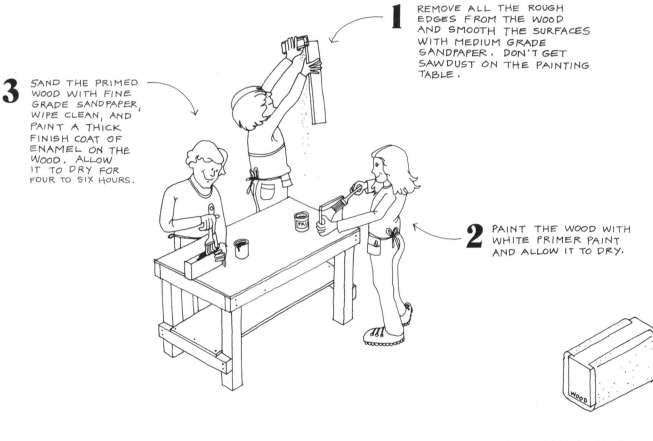

1 REMOVE ALL THE ROUGH EDGES FROM THE WOOD AND SMOOTH THE SURFACES WITH MEDIUM GRADE SANDPAPER. DON'T GET SAWDUST ON THE PAINTING TABLE.

3 SAND THE PRIMED WOOD WITH FINE GRADE SANDPAPER, WIPE CLEAN, AND PAINT A THICK FINISH COAT OF ENAMEL ON THE WOOD. ALLOW IT TO DRY FOR FOUR TO SIX HOURS.

2 PAINT THE WOOD WITH WHITE PRIMER PAINT AND ALLOW IT TO DRY.

MAKE A SANDING BLOCK WITH A PIECE OF SANDPAPER WRAPPED AROUND A BLOCK OF WOOD.

Jess painting the finished coat over a primed piece of plywood.

Building Your Workshop

This chapter is devoted to helping you set up a pleasant, well-ordered place to work. If you plan to take your carpentry seriously, you'll need a strong workbench with a vise, a toolbox to carry your tools, and at least two sturdy sawhorses. These are the basic workshop necessities that will help you become a carpenter.

Simple step-by-step plans for the complete workshop begin on the next page. As you build it, take your time and try to perfect your skills in sawing and hammering, so that when you begin building the projects, you'll be a good, confident carpenter.

Adam and Molly with the finished toolbox.

The Site

Your building site will be the place where you set up your workshop. It'll be the center of activity for everything that relates to your carpentry, so it should be chosen with care. It should be close enough to a road or driveway so that you don't have to carry heavy materials long distances, and in a spot that doesn't interfere with another's activities, such as your mother's flower garden. You'll need an open area at least 10' square, giving you ample space to store materials and build your projects.

Once you've established the location of your site, trim any low branches and rake the ground as clean as possible to prevent lost tools and nails and poison ivy.

Set up the orange crates mentioned in Chapter One to act as a temporary work table (to build the workbench) and lay out the clear plastic sheet to serve as protection for your building materials.

Molly and Adam arranging the orange crates, and Ben and Jess clearing the site.

Building Your Workbench

The most important part of your workshop will be a good, solid workbench. It'll provide the surface upon which all of your projects will be built, so it's important that you take your time and carefully follow the directions to construct it properly.

Assembling the Tools and Materials

Below is a list of tools and materials needed to build your workbench. Until you have time to build your toolbox, you can temporarily keep the tools in an orange crate to carry them and guard against misplacing them. Store your materials flat, and cover them from bad weather.

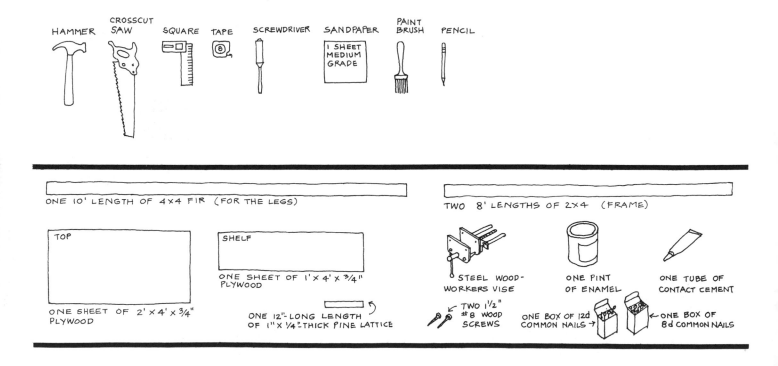

HAMMER CROSSCUT SAW SQUARE TAPE SCREWDRIVER SANDPAPER (I SHEET MEDIUM GRADE) PAINT BRUSH PENCIL

ONE 10' LENGTH OF 4X4 FIR (FOR THE LEGS)

TWO 8' LENGTHS OF 2X4 (FRAME)

TOP — ONE SHEET OF 2' X 4' X 3/4" PLYWOOD

SHELF — ONE SHEET OF 1' X 4' X 3/4" PLYWOOD

ONE 12"-LONG LENGTH OF 1" X 1/4"-THICK PINE LATTICE

STEEL WOOD-WORKERS VISE

ONE PINT OF ENAMEL

ONE TUBE OF CONTACT CEMENT

TWO 1 1/2" #8 WOOD SCREWS

ONE BOX OF 12d COMMON NAILS →

← ONE BOX OF 8d COMMON NAILS

Molly and Jess checking the tools, Ben tying his carpentry apron, and Adam unloading the materials.

Sawing the Parts

Below are instructions for sawing all the wooden parts you'll need to build your workbench. Make sure you make sharp, dark pencil lines so that they're easy to follow when sawing.

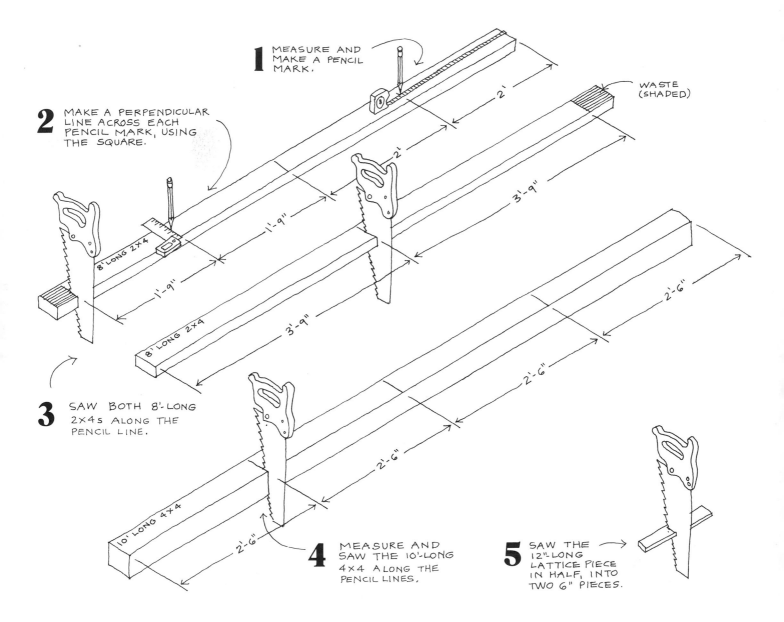

1 MEASURE AND MAKE A PENCIL MARK.

WASTE (SHADED)

2 MAKE A PERPENDICULAR LINE ACROSS EACH PENCIL MARK, USING THE SQUARE.

8' LONG 2×4

2'

2'

1'-9"

3'-9"

1'-9"

8' LONG 2×4

3'-9"

3 SAW BOTH 8'-LONG 2×4s ALONG THE PENCIL LINE.

2'-6"

2'-6"

10' LONG 4×4

2'-6"

2'-6"

4 MEASURE AND SAW THE 10'-LONG 4×4 ALONG THE PENCIL LINES.

5 SAW THE 12"-LONG LATTICE PIECE IN HALF, INTO TWO 6" PIECES.

Molly measuring a 2x4, and Jess and Ben sawing the 4x4.

Assembling the Parts

Below are five steps required to build your workbench. It's important that the nails are hammered straight. If they're not, your workbench will be weak. So, ask a friend to watch to see if the nails are going in straight as you hammer them. If they're crooked, pull them out and start again. Have patience.

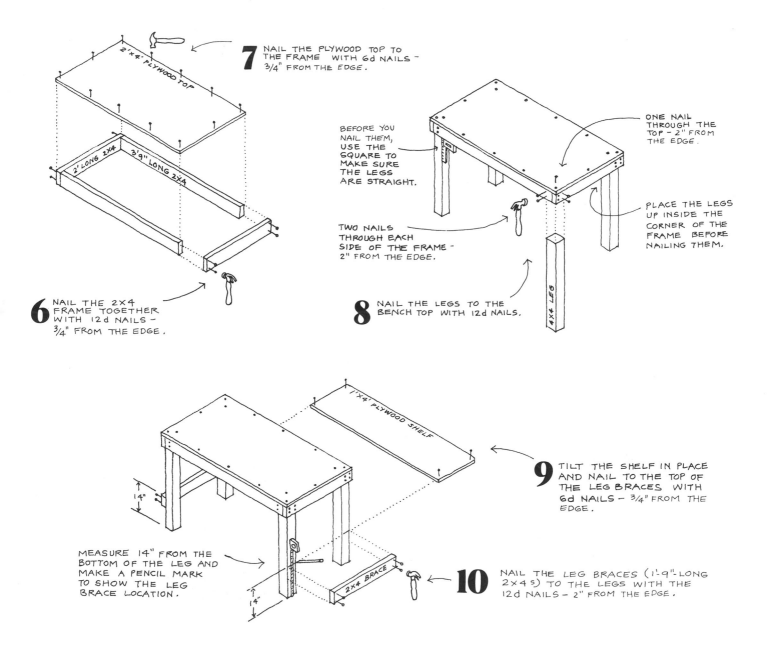

7 NAIL THE PLYWOOD TOP TO THE FRAME WITH 6d NAILS – 3/4" FROM THE EDGE.

2'×4'-PLYWOOD TOP

2' LONG 2×4   3'9" LONG 2×4

6 NAIL THE 2×4 FRAME TOGETHER WITH 12d NAILS – 3/4" FROM THE EDGE.

BEFORE YOU NAIL THEM, USE THE SQUARE TO MAKE SURE THE LEGS ARE STRAIGHT.

TWO NAILS THROUGH EACH SIDE OF THE FRAME – 2" FROM THE EDGE.

ONE NAIL THROUGH THE TOP – 2" FROM THE EDGE.

PLACE THE LEGS UP INSIDE THE CORNER OF THE FRAME BEFORE NAILING THEM.

4×4 LEG

8 NAIL THE LEGS TO THE BENCH TOP WITH 12d NAILS.

1'×4' PLYWOOD SHELF

9 TILT THE SHELF IN PLACE AND NAIL TO THE TOP OF THE LEG BRACES WITH 6d NAILS – 3/4" FROM THE EDGE.

MEASURE 14" FROM THE BOTTOM OF THE LEG AND MAKE A PENCIL MARK TO SHOW THE LEG BRACE LOCATION.

14"

14"

2×4 BRACE

10 NAIL THE LEG BRACES (1'-9"-LONG 2×4s) TO THE LEGS WITH THE 12d NAILS – 2" FROM THE EDGE.

50

Adam hammering the nails to secure a leg. Ben and Jess steadying the work. Molly has the fourth leg ready.

Finishing the Job

You'll want to give your workbench top two or three coats of enamel paint to make the surface weatherproof and easy to clean. Make sure each coat is dry before painting the next one. Follow the instructions below to install the vise.

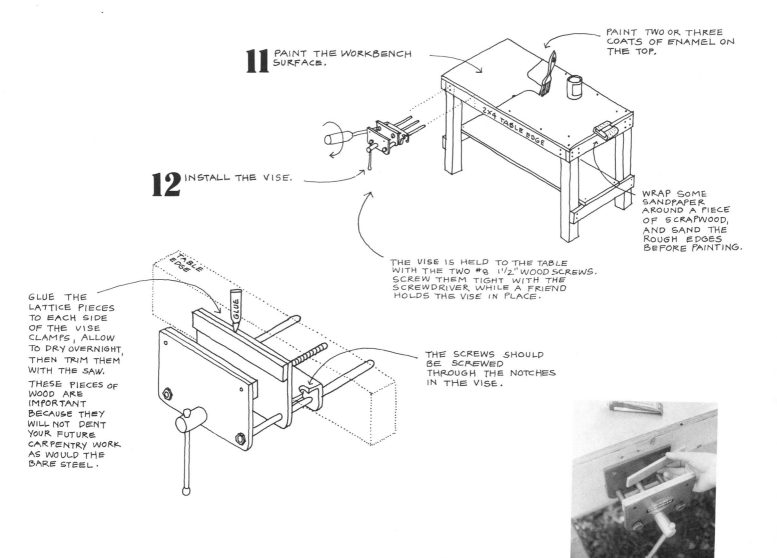

11 PAINT THE WORKBENCH SURFACE.

PAINT TWO OR THREE COATS OF ENAMEL ON THE TOP.

2X4 TABLE EDGE

12 INSTALL THE VISE.

WRAP SOME SANDPAPER AROUND A PIECE OF SCRAPWOOD, AND SAND THE ROUGH EDGES BEFORE PAINTING.

THE VISE IS HELD TO THE TABLE WITH THE TWO #8 1½" WOOD SCREWS. SCREW THEM TIGHT WITH THE SCREWDRIVER WHILE A FRIEND HOLDS THE VISE IN PLACE.

TABLE EDGE

GLUE

GLUE THE LATTICE PIECES TO EACH SIDE OF THE VISE CLAMPS, ALLOW TO DRY OVERNIGHT, THEN TRIM THEM WITH THE SAW.

THESE PIECES OF WOOD ARE IMPORTANT BECAUSE THEY WILL NOT DENT YOUR FUTURE CARPENTRY WORK AS WOULD THE BARE STEEL.

THE SCREWS SHOULD BE SCREWED THROUGH THE NOTCHES IN THE VISE.

Gluing the lattice to the vise.

Adam and Jess screwing the vise to the table, Molly putting in the shelf, and Ben painting the top.

Building Your Toolbox

What is a carpenter without a well-built toolbox? If you follow the plans, beginning below, and are careful with your sawing, hammering, and drilling, you'll have a beautiful toolbox to carry your tools from your outdoor workshop to your house.

Assembling the Tools and Materials

Here are the tools and materials you'll need. Make sure the 1x8 board is straight and true — not warped (curved) — when you buy it. Then, make sure you keep it dry so that it doesn't warp. This'll insure that your toolbox is square and easy to build.

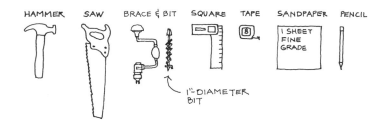

HAMMER SAW BRACE & BIT SQUARE TAPE SANDPAPER PENCIL

I SHEET FINE GRADE

1"-DIAMETER BIT

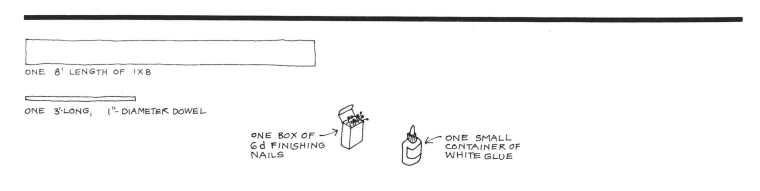

ONE 8' LENGTH OF 1X8

ONE 3'-LONG, 1"-DIAMETER DOWEL

ONE BOX OF 6d FINISHING NAILS

ONE SMALL CONTAINER OF WHITE GLUE

Molly and Jess getting the tools ready. Adam and Ben setting up the lumber.

Sawing the Parts

The seven steps for sawing all the wooden parts
needed to build your toolbox are shown on this and
the facing page. Remember, you need two side pieces,
two end pieces, and one bottom piece, all cut from the
1x8 board. Take care to make your saw cuts as
straight as possible, so that your toolbox will fit
together well.

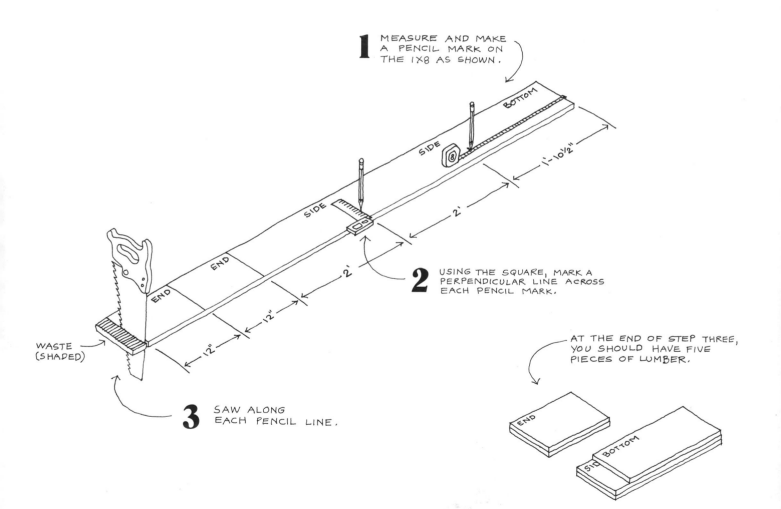

1 MEASURE AND MAKE A PENCIL MARK ON THE 1X8 AS SHOWN.

2 USING THE SQUARE, MARK A PERPENDICULAR LINE ACROSS EACH PENCIL MARK.

3 SAW ALONG EACH PENCIL LINE.

WASTE (SHADED)

AT THE END OF STEP THREE, YOU SHOULD HAVE FIVE PIECES OF LUMBER.

Follow the instructions below to saw the end pieces in the proper shape. Use the vise to hold each piece as you trim off the corners with the saw.

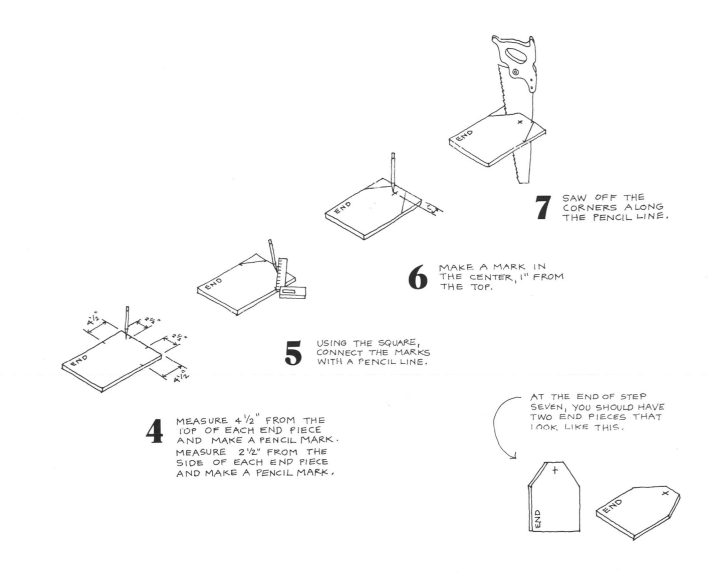

7 SAW OFF THE CORNERS ALONG THE PENCIL LINE.

6 MAKE A MARK IN THE CENTER, 1" FROM THE TOP.

5 USING THE SQUARE, CONNECT THE MARKS WITH A PENCIL LINE.

4 MEASURE 4½" FROM THE TOP OF EACH END PIECE AND MAKE A PENCIL MARK. MEASURE 2½" FROM THE SIDE OF EACH END PIECE AND MAKE A PENCIL MARK.

AT THE END OF STEP SEVEN, YOU SHOULD HAVE TWO END PIECES THAT LOOK LIKE THIS.

Drilling the Parts

Use the vise to hold the two end pieces as you drill the handle holes. Make sure to drill carefully until the drill pierces the wood, then turn the piece around and drill from the other side. This procedure is explained on page 32 and will give you a clean, professional-looking drilled hole.

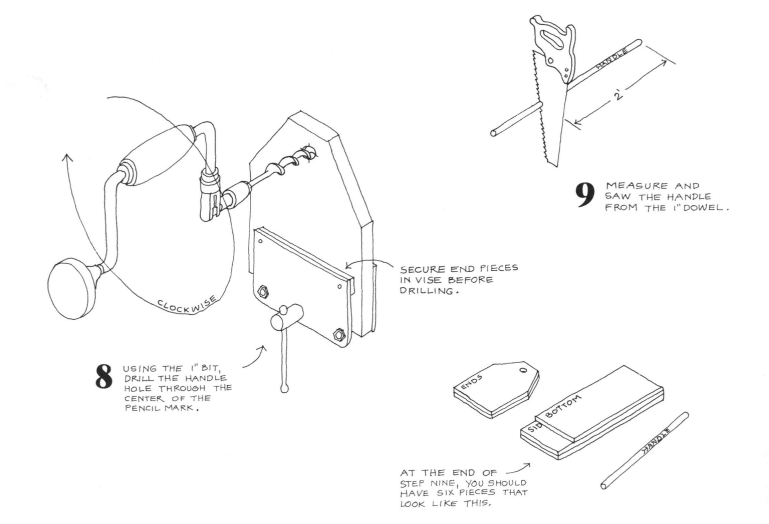

9 MEASURE AND SAW THE HANDLE FROM THE 1" DOWEL.

SECURE END PIECES IN VISE BEFORE DRILLING.

CLOCKWISE

8 USING THE 1" BIT, DRILL THE HANDLE HOLE THROUGH THE CENTER OF THE PENCIL MARK.

AT THE END OF STEP NINE, YOU SHOULD HAVE SIX PIECES THAT LOOK LIKE THIS.

Adam drilling the end pieces. Ben and Jess sawing the sides and bottom.

Assembling the Parts

Before you nail your toolbox together, hold the parts against each other to make sure they fit well. It's easy to fix a mistake before the pieces are nailed together. Once you're sure that everything is perfect, sand the parts with fine sandpaper and nail them together according to the three steps shown below.

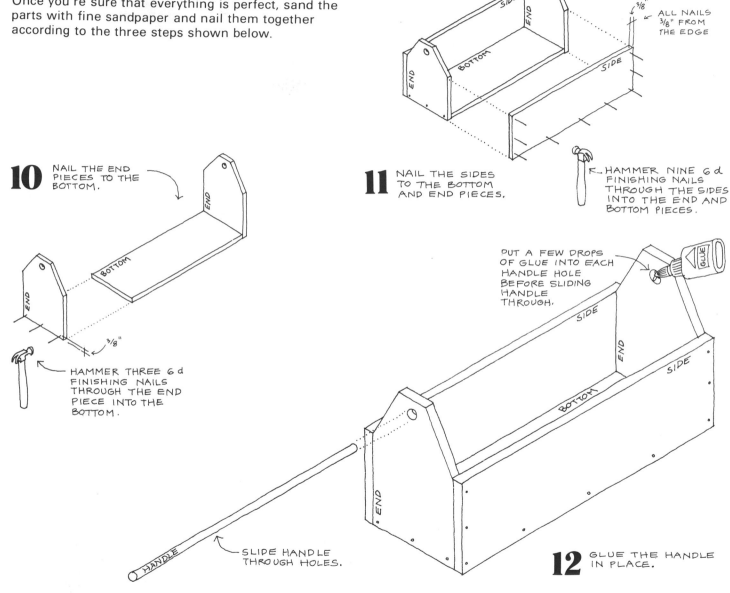

10 NAIL THE END PIECES TO THE BOTTOM.

HAMMER THREE 6d FINISHING NAILS THROUGH THE END PIECE INTO THE BOTTOM.

11 NAIL THE SIDES TO THE BOTTOM AND END PIECES.

3/8" ALL NAILS 3/8" FROM THE EDGE

HAMMER NINE 6d FINISHING NAILS THROUGH THE SIDES INTO THE END AND BOTTOM PIECES.

PUT A FEW DROPS OF GLUE INTO EACH HANDLE HOLE BEFORE SLIDING HANDLE THROUGH.

SLIDE HANDLE THROUGH HOLES.

12 GLUE THE HANDLE IN PLACE.

The toolbox will be finished when Jess and Ben nail on the side and Molly glues the handle in the holes.

61

Building Your Sawhorses

To complete your workshop, you'll need a set of sawhorses — so named because they look like horses (four legs) and are used by carpenters for sawing. They don't require as much accuracy as the workbench or toolbox, but they must be strong. Nailing straight, unbent nails is important.

Assembling the Tools and Materials

Below are the tools and materials you'll need to build two sawhorses. Try to get 2x4s that are unwarped (uncurved) and have as few knots as possible.

HAMMER SAW SQUARE TAPE SANDPAPER PENCIL

TWO 10' LENGTHS OF 2×4

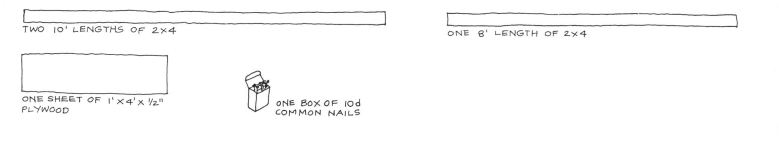

ONE 8' LENGTH OF 2×4

ONE SHEET OF 1' × 4' × ½"
PLYWOOD

ONE BOX OF 10d
COMMON NAILS

It's good practice to cover your materials with a plastic tarp after you get them to your workshop site so that they don't warp from damp weather. It's almost impossible to work with warped wood.

Sawing the Parts

The next three pages show the nine steps to follow to saw the wooden parts necessary to build two sawhorses. There's a lot of sawing to be done, so you'll have to work hard and keep your patience.

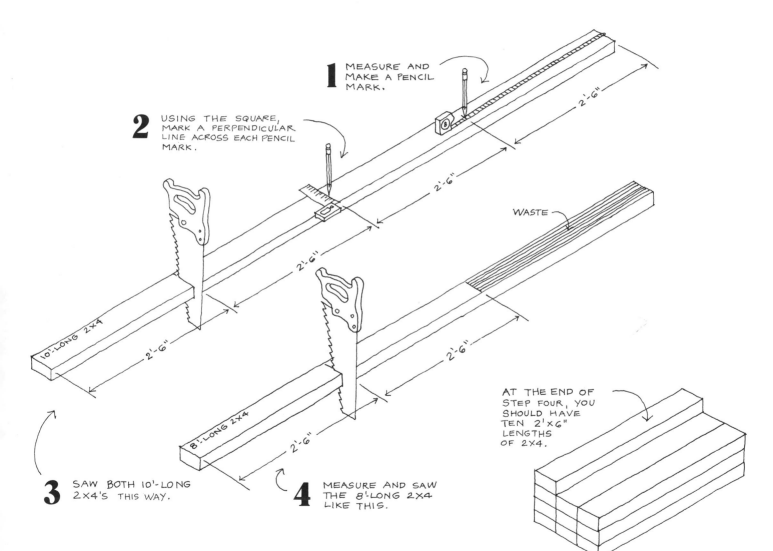

1 MEASURE AND MAKE A PENCIL MARK.

2 USING THE SQUARE, MARK A PERPENDICULAR LINE ACROSS EACH PENCIL MARK.

2'-6"

2'-6"

2'-6"

WASTE

10'-LONG 2X4

2'-6"

8'-LONG 2X4

2'-6"

2'-6"

AT THE END OF STEP FOUR, YOU SHOULD HAVE TEN 2'X6" LENGTHS OF 2X4.

3 SAW BOTH 10'-LONG 2X4'S THIS WAY.

4 MEASURE AND SAW THE 8'-LONG 2X4 LIKE THIS.

The hardest part in making the sawhorses is trimming the eight legs so they slope. If you keep the saw in a straight up-and-down position, as shown in step six, and carefully saw along the pencil line, your cuts should be perfect.

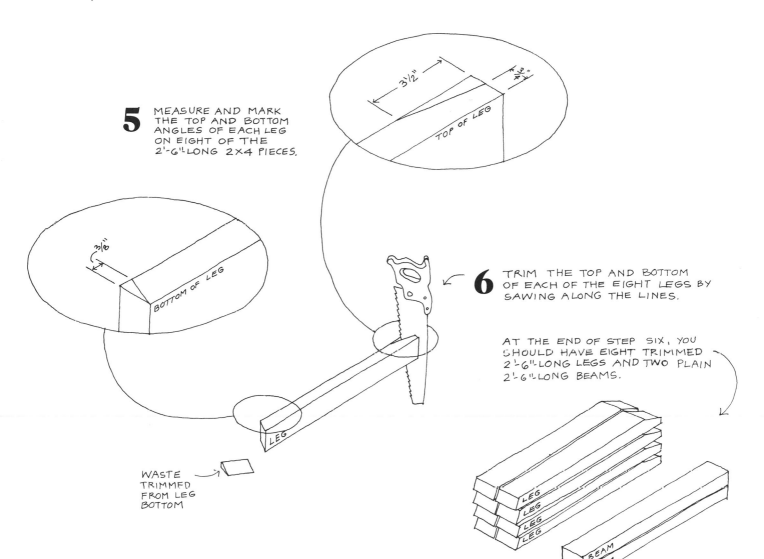

5 MEASURE AND MARK THE TOP AND BOTTOM ANGLES OF EACH LEG ON EIGHT OF THE 2'-6"-LONG 2×4 PIECES.

3½"

¾"

TOP OF LEG

⅜"

BOTTOM OF LEG

6 TRIM THE TOP AND BOTTOM OF EACH OF THE EIGHT LEGS BY SAWING ALONG THE LINES.

AT THE END OF STEP SIX, YOU SHOULD HAVE EIGHT TRIMMED 2'-6"-LONG LEGS AND TWO PLAIN 2'-6"-LONG BEAMS.

LEG

WASTE TRIMMED FROM LEG BOTTOM

LEG
LEG
LEG
LEG

BEAM
BEAM

The strength of the sawhorse comes from the plywood end pieces. If you turn to the next page, you'll see how the end pieces are used to make the finished sawhorse strong. Below are instructions for laying out and sawing these end pieces from the piece of 1'x4'x½" plywood.

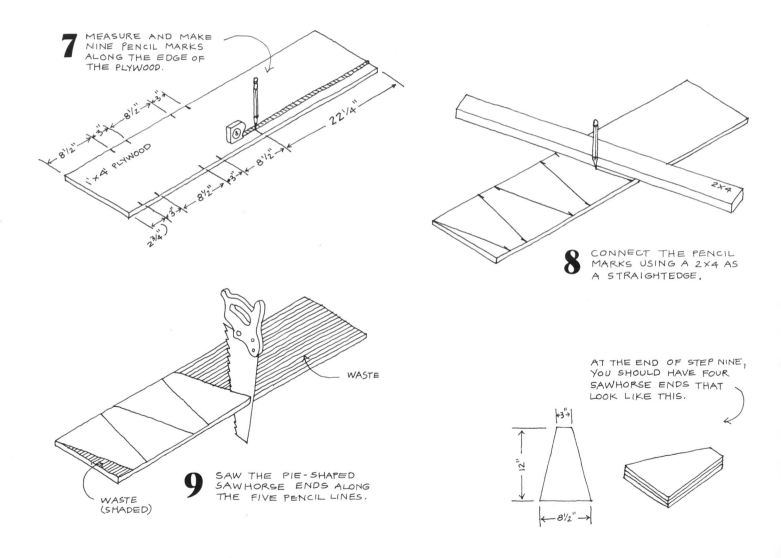

7 MEASURE AND MAKE NINE PENCIL MARKS ALONG THE EDGE OF THE PLYWOOD.

1'x4' PLYWOOD

22¼"

8½" 3" 8½" 3"

8½" 3" 8½"

2¾"

8 CONNECT THE PENCIL MARKS USING A 2×4 AS A STRAIGHTEDGE.

2×4

WASTE

WASTE (SHADED)

9 SAW THE PIE-SHAPED SAWHORSE ENDS ALONG THE FIVE PENCIL LINES.

AT THE END OF STEP NINE, YOU SHOULD HAVE FOUR SAWHORSE ENDS THAT LOOK LIKE THIS.

3"

12"

8½"

Adam trimming the legs. Jess laying out the ends, and Ben and Molly sawing the 2x4 parts.

Assembling the Parts

Below are the two steps to follow to make the sawhorses. Have someone hold the parts together on the workbench, as shown in the photograph on the opposite page, while you nail them together.

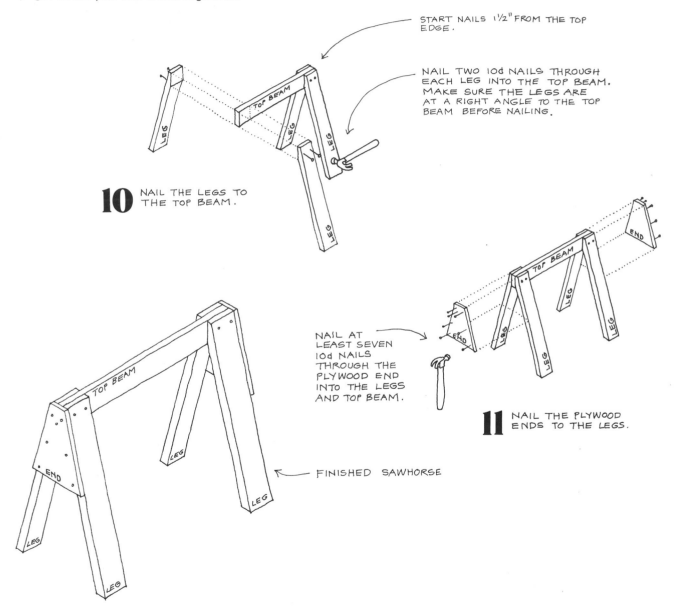

START NAILS 1½" FROM THE TOP EDGE.

NAIL TWO 10d NAILS THROUGH EACH LEG INTO THE TOP BEAM. MAKE SURE THE LEGS ARE AT A RIGHT ANGLE TO THE TOP BEAM BEFORE NAILING.

10 NAIL THE LEGS TO THE TOP BEAM.

NAIL AT LEAST SEVEN 10d NAILS THROUGH THE PLYWOOD END INTO THE LEGS AND TOP BEAM.

11 NAIL THE PLYWOOD ENDS TO THE LEGS.

FINISHED SAWHORSE

Adam and Molly nailing on the legs. Jess and Ben finishing the job by nailing on the end pieces.

Celebration

After you've finished your workshop, you'll have completed a great deal of hard work. After you've driven the last nail, you may simply want to jump for joy, or you might want to have a party. Whatever you decide, you deserve to celebrate. Now you're ready to use your new workshop to build the projects.

The new shop is finished! Time to build the projects.

One-Day Projects

One-Day Projects

Now that you've learned how to use all the tools, and you've built a strong, efficient workshop, you're ready to build the project(s).

First, of course, you must choose which project you like from those four pictured on the facing page. They are arranged in order of difficulty: tugboat, block set, birdhouse, and candle chandelier. If you want to build the easiest project first, start with the tugboat. Before you begin, however, it's a good idea to become familiar with all four projects by studying what will be required of you to build each one. Carefully read pages 74 to 111, then choose your starting project.

Each project is designed to be completed in one day, so if you work with a friend or friends, you should be able to finish each in a matter of hours. Remember, if you paint the birdhouse and the candle chandelier (as suggested), they'll need to dry overnight.

Do your best work, and good luck.

WHY NOT BUILD
ALL FOUR ?

Tugboat

Birdhouse

Block Set

Candle Chandelier

Tugboat

The tugboat is probably the most commonly built carpentry project of children around the world since it's built with wood scraps and can be used in a bathtub or a stream or pond.

Our tugboat is designed to begin developing sawing and drilling techniques. A few simple crosscut saw cuts, four drilled holes, five minutes of careful nailing, and your boat is ready for sailing.

Remember to thoroughly read all the instructions before you begin. The task you're performing will always be done better if you know what's next.

Assembling the Tools and Materials

Here's a list of tools and materials needed to build your tugboat. Get them ready before you start.

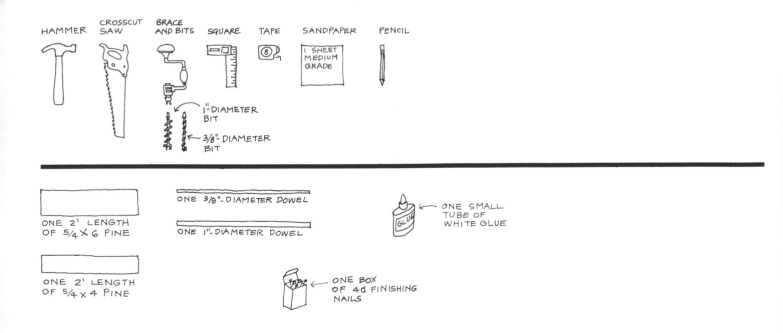

Ben setting up the materials. Adam gathering the tools.

Sawing the Parts

Below are the four simple steps for sawing and two steps for drilling the parts you'll need to build your tugboat. Try to keep your saw cuts straight, and drill your holes *halfway* through the wood. The holes are meant to hold the dowels, so a simple ½"-deep hole is necessary. Pay particular attention to the photographs on the facing page — Adam and Ben are building the tugboat correctly.

1 MEASURE AND SAW THE TWO CABIN PIECES FROM THE 2' LENGTH OF 5/4 × 4 PINE.

2 MEASURE AND SAW THE BOAT BASE FROM THE 2' LENGTH OF 5/4 × 6 PINE.

THE FRONT OF THE BOAT COMES TO A POINT.

3 MEASURE AND SAW TWO 4"-HIGH SMOKE-STACKS FROM THE 1" DOWEL.

4 MEASURE AND SAW TWO 1½"-HIGH ANCHOR POSTS FROM THE 3/8" DOWEL.

5 DRILL TWO CENTERED, 3/8"-DIAMETER HOLES (½" DEEP) FOR THE ANCHOR POSTS, 1" FROM EACH END OF THE BASE.

6 DRILL TWO CENTERED, 1"-DIAMETER HOLES FOR THE SMOKE-STACKS IN THE CABIN TOP.

HOLD YOUR WORK STEADY WITH THE VISE.

Ben sawing the base.

Adam sanding the base. Ben drilling the smokestack holes.

Assembling the Parts

The most fun of this project is assembling into a beautiful tugboat the parts that you've just sawed and drilled. Before doing this, however, you should sand each piece so that all the rough edges are removed and the wood gains a nice smooth finish.

Take your time, especially with the nailing. Make sure your nails are at least ⅜" from the edge, or you may split the wood. Be sure that the smokestacks and anchor posts are glued straight.

8 NAIL THE CABIN TOP TO THE CABIN BOTTOM WITH TWO 4d FINISHING NAILS.

OPTIONAL STRING FOR ANCHORING

7 NAIL THE CABIN BOTTOM TO THE BASE WITH TWO 4d FINISHING NAILS.

9 PUT A FEW DROPS OF WHITE GLUE INSIDE EACH OF THE FOUR HOLES AND INSERT THE FOUR DOWELS.

Ben and Adam gluing the dowels into their holes.

Launching

The tugboat is great fun in a bathtub, swimming pool, or any natural body of water, but it's really designed for streams. When launched upstream, it'll go downstream with the flow of the water, occasionally crashing into rocks, running over leaves, and scaring a fish or two. If you make two boats, they can race, and, of course, there's much fun to be had with a fleet of several boats.

Adam and Ben launching their tugboat in a stream.

NOT BAD.

Block Set

The block set is probably the oldest toy and is one with which children of all ages can play. The best part about it is that it can be made from wood scraps, so it's very inexpensive. Consider making two or three sets so that you've enough blocks to build giant castles.

Making the block set improves your sawing and drilling skills. If you don't make straight saw cuts, the blocks won't work as well as they should. And if you don't drill straight, clean holes, the dowels won't fit as well as they should. If your carpentry work is good, your block set will work well.

Assembling the Tools and Materials

Here's a list of tools and materials needed to build your block set.

CROSSCUT SAW

BRACE AND BIT

SQUARE

TAPE

SANDPAPER

1 SHEET FINE GRADE

PENCIL

← 1" DIAMETER BIT

ONE 4' LENGTH OF 5/4 × 4

ONE 1" DIAMETER DOWEL

Ben and Adam getting the tools and materials ready to build the block set.

Laying Out the Parts

As you may recall, on page 20 we discussed that when a 2x4 piece of lumber is kiln dried (all the lumber used in this book should be kiln dried), it shrinks to 1½"x3½". Even though it's really 1½"x3½", it's still referred to as a "two by four" or 2x4. Well, the piece that we are using to make the block set must also shrink from 1¼"x4" to 1"x3½" when it is kiln dried. This is important because if we want to make square blocks, we must make them 3½"x3½".

This is the reason for the layout in step one below: seven squares that are 3½"x3½" and three rectangles of 7"x3½", which are twice the size of the squares. Be careful measuring, as you don't want to make mistakes and waste lumber.

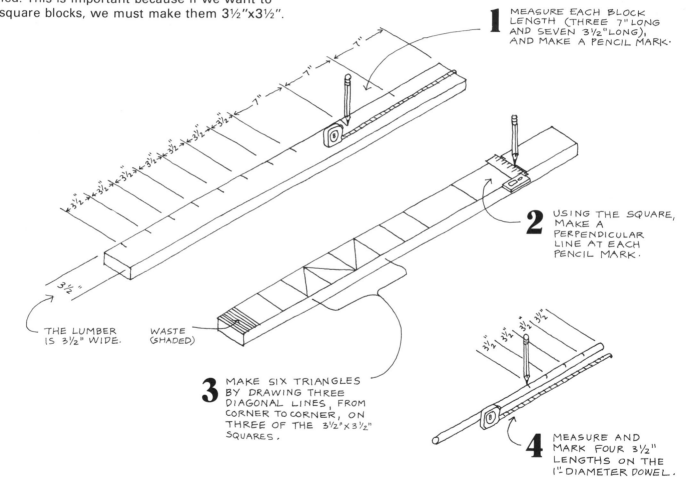

1 MEASURE EACH BLOCK LENGTH (THREE 7" LONG AND SEVEN 3½" LONG), AND MAKE A PENCIL MARK.

2 USING THE SQUARE, MAKE A PERPENDICULAR LINE AT EACH PENCIL MARK.

THE LUMBER IS 3½" WIDE.

WASTE (SHADED)

3 MAKE SIX TRIANGLES BY DRAWING THREE DIAGONAL LINES, FROM CORNER TO CORNER, ON THREE OF THE 3½"x3½" SQUARES.

4 MEASURE AND MARK FOUR 3½" LENGTHS ON THE 1"-DIAMETER DOWEL.

Using the square, Adam draws perpendicular lines across the lumber.

Sawing the Parts

Since a block set depends on balance, you must make perfect saw cuts. Carefully saw along the perpendicular lines you've drawn. Try to get a friend to watch you to make sure that you're sawing straight up and down (perpendicular to the ground).

The more cuts you make, the better your saw cuts will be, so you might want to measure a few extra blocks in case you make mistakes. In this case, you'll need a

6'- or 8'-long piece of 5/4x4 lumber. The more blocks you make, the more fun your block set will be. But you must be patient and saw carefully and true, or your block set will have crazy angles and won't balance as you would like it to.

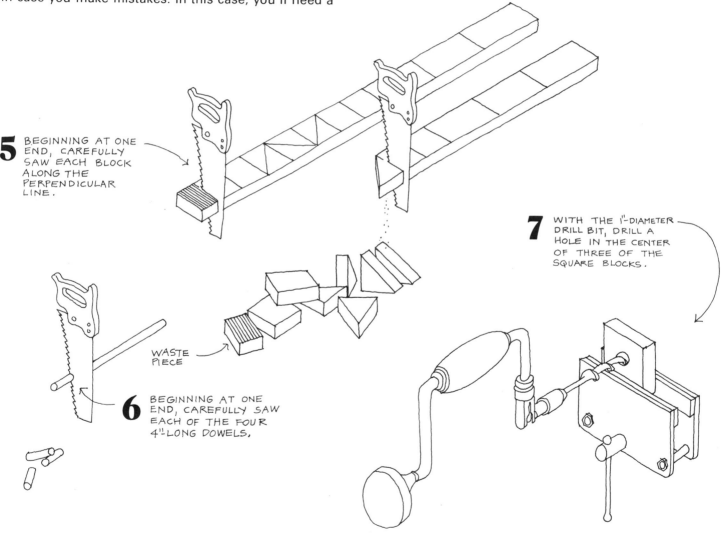

5 BEGINNING AT ONE END, CAREFULLY SAW EACH BLOCK ALONG THE PERPENDICULAR LINE.

WASTE PIECE

6 BEGINNING AT ONE END, CAREFULLY SAW EACH OF THE FOUR 4"-LONG DOWELS.

7 WITH THE 1"-DIAMETER DRILL BIT, DRILL A HOLE IN THE CENTER OF THREE OF THE SQUARE BLOCKS.

Adam sawing the blocks, and Ben sawing the dowels.

Sanding and Building

Before you start building castles with your blocks, you should carefully sand each one with fine sandpaper. Sanding may seem tedious and boring, but it's a necessary task to complete a good carpentry job. You don't want splinters, so set aside thirty minutes or so to do a good sanding job.

A good set of blocks is a toy that can be left permanently on a coffee table or desk, to be played with by all members and friends of the family. You'll be surprised what great castles — or whatever — your mom or dad or grandparents will make while they're sitting and talking.

You'll also be surprised at the compliments you'll get when they realize you made the blocks.

Adam sanding the block edges, and Ben building a castle.

Birdhouse

The birdhouse has been a traditional carpentry project of children for decades. If you enjoy watching wildlife, especially birds, this project is a good one for you.

Our birdhouse develops skills in sawing, drilling, nailing, and painting. After you've completed it, you'll want to hang it near a window, put some birdseed on its front porch, and, if you're lucky, you'll see it attracts birds looking for a spot to make a nest.

Remember to read the complete instructions until you understand them. Be as neat and careful as you can. Don't allow yourself to hammer a crooked nail or saw a crooked line. You're teaching yourself to be a good carpenter.

Assembling the Tools and Materials

Here's a list of the tools and materials you'll need to build your birdhouse. It's best to gather all of them in your workshop before you begin.

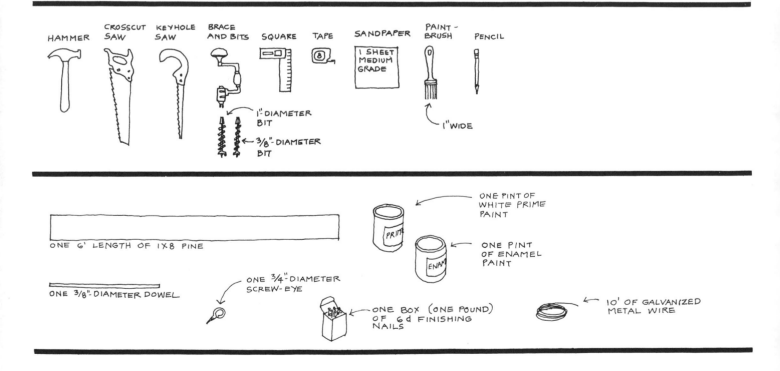

Ben and Jess checking the tools. Adam assembling the lumber.

Sawing the Parts

Seven steps for laying out and sawing all the wooden parts needed to build your birdhouse are shown on this and the facing page. Double-check your measurements before sawing to make sure you don't make any mistakes.

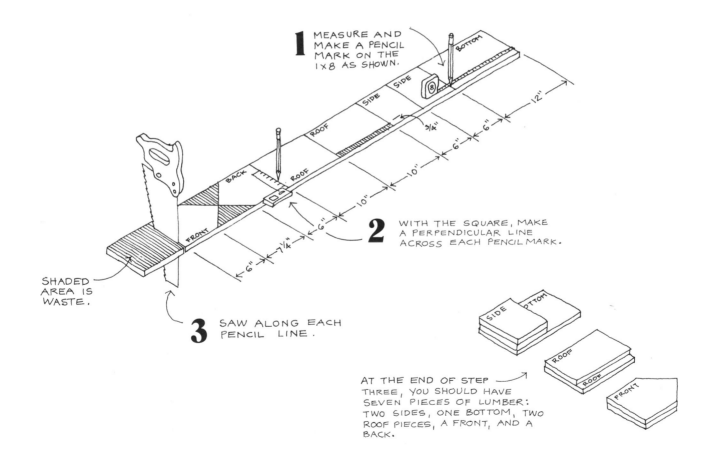

1 MEASURE AND MAKE A PENCIL MARK ON THE 1 x 8 AS SHOWN.

2 WITH THE SQUARE, MAKE A PERPENDICULAR LINE ACROSS EACH PENCIL MARK.

3 SAW ALONG EACH PENCIL LINE.

SHADED AREA IS WASTE.

AT THE END OF STEP THREE, YOU SHOULD HAVE SEVEN PIECES OF LUMBER: TWO SIDES, ONE BOTTOM, TWO ROOF PIECES, A FRONT, AND A BACK.

Follow steps four, five, and six to lay out the door and windows of the front and back pieces of the birdhouse. Use the square as a straightedge to make your pencil lines.

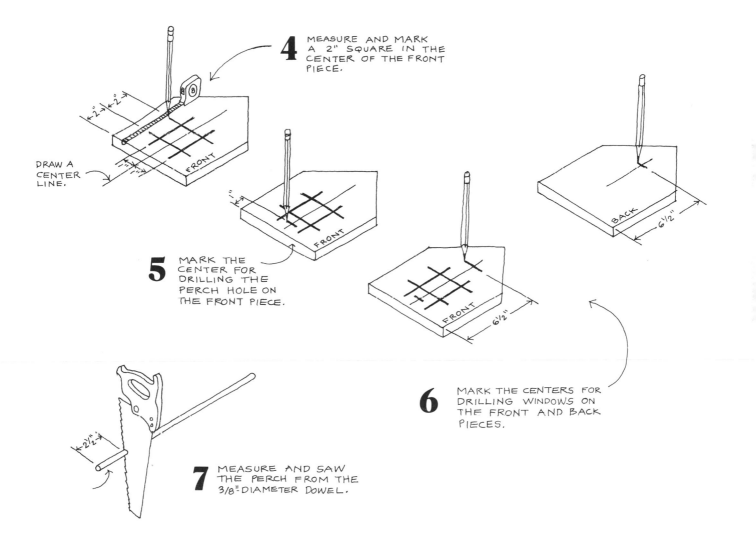

4 MEASURE AND MARK A 2" SQUARE IN THE CENTER OF THE FRONT PIECE.

DRAW A CENTER LINE.

5 MARK THE CENTER FOR DRILLING THE PERCH HOLE ON THE FRONT PIECE.

6 MARK THE CENTERS FOR DRILLING WINDOWS ON THE FRONT AND BACK PIECES.

7 MEASURE AND SAW THE PERCH FROM THE 3/8" DIAMETER DOWEL.

Drilling the Parts

Use the vise to hold the front and back pieces as you drill the window, door, and perch holes. Drill carefully until the drill bit pierces the wood, then turn the piece around and drill from the other side. This procedure will take some extra time but will give you smooth holes. Sand all the pieces after you've keyhole-sawed the door from the front piece.

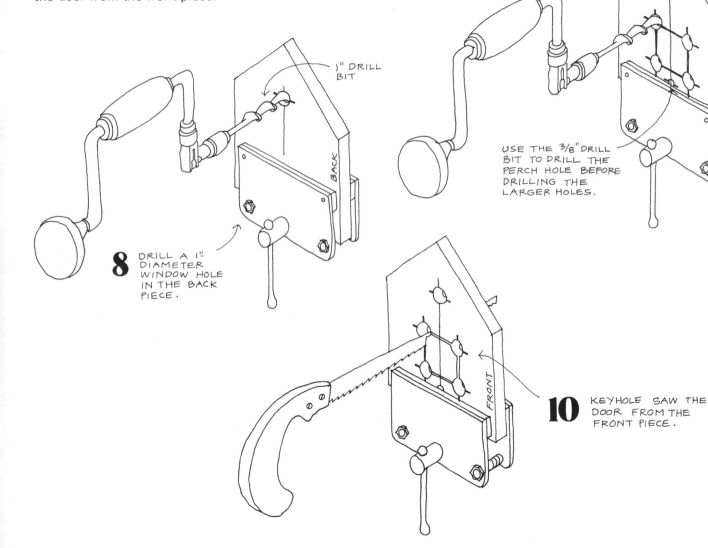

9 DRILL A 1"-DIAMETER WINDOW HOLE AND FOUR 1"-DIAMETER HOLES (SO THE KEYHOLE SAW CAN CUT THE DOOR) IN THE FRONT PIECE.

WINDOW HOLE

1" DRILL BIT

USE THE 3/8" DRILL BIT TO DRILL THE PERCH HOLE BEFORE DRILLING THE LARGER HOLES.

8 DRILL A 1" DIAMETER WINDOW HOLE IN THE BACK PIECE.

10 KEYHOLE SAW THE DOOR FROM THE FRONT PIECE.

Ben keyhole-sawing the birdhouse entrance.

Assembling the Parts

Follow the instructions below to assemble your birdhouse. Before you nail them, hold the pieces together to make sure they fit properly. Remember to drive the nails straight. If a nail starts going crooked, pull it out and start another one in a different spot. Good nailing will insure a strong birdhouse.

Paint the roof a color of your choice with a thick coat of enamel paint over a coat of white primer paint that has been allowed to dry thoroughly. This will weatherproof your birdhouse and give you a chance to use your painting skills.

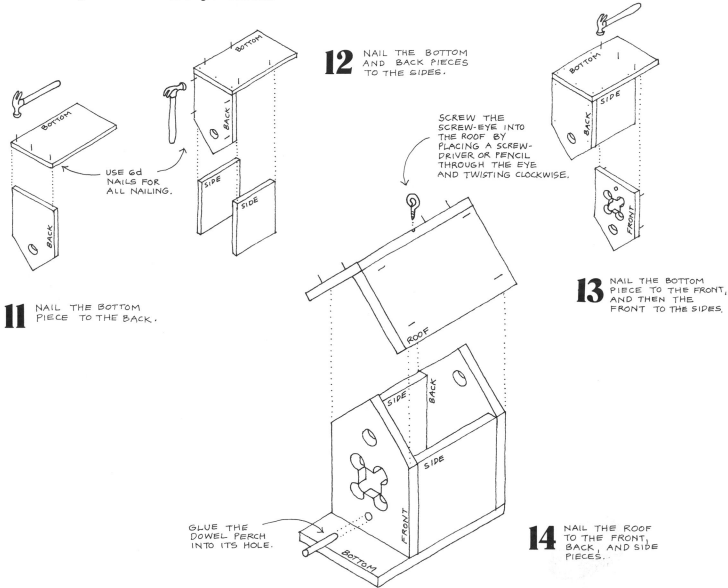

USE 6d NAILS FOR ALL NAILING.

11 NAIL THE BOTTOM PIECE TO THE BACK.

12 NAIL THE BOTTOM AND BACK PIECES TO THE SIDES.

SCREW THE SCREW-EYE INTO THE ROOF BY PLACING A SCREW-DRIVER OR PENCIL THROUGH THE EYE AND TWISTING CLOCKWISE.

13 NAIL THE BOTTOM PIECE TO THE FRONT, AND THEN THE FRONT TO THE SIDES.

GLUE THE DOWEL PERCH INTO ITS HOLE.

14 NAIL THE ROOF TO THE FRONT, BACK, AND SIDE PIECES.

98

Jess nailing the back to the sides.

Jess nailing the front piece to the sides.

Jess nailing the roof to the birdhouse.

Jess painting the roof. Ben inserting the screw eye.

Finishing the Job

Use some galvanized wire or strong nylon cord to hang the birdhouse from a tree limb. Hang it far enough from the tree trunk so that squirrels can't get to the birdseed. Make sure the wire or string connections around the limb and through the birdhouse screw-eye are strong, so the birdhouse doesn't blow down in a heavy wind.

Put some birdseed on the birdhouse front porch, sit back, admire your handiwork, and hope that some lucky birds decide to build a nest and raise a family in your birdhouse.

IF I WERE A BIRD, THIS IS WHERE I'D LIVE.

Jess and Ben hanging the birdhouse.

Adam and Molly studying a nest.

Candle Chandelier

The candle chandelier is something that makes a great gift for your parents, grandparents, or a special friend. As you know, candlelight is very soft and romantic, so many people use it to light their dining table. In fact, candle chandeliers were quite popular before electricity. Our chandelier holds eight candles, and, when they are lit, they give the room a beautiful warm glow.

Care must be taken when lighting the candles — matches are always dangerous — otherwise, except for the drilling, this is a relatively simple project.

Assembling the Tools and Materials

Below is a list of tools and materials you'll need to make the candle chandelier. The wooden spindle can be purchased at most home centers or lumberyards in various designs and sizes. Choose one that is about

14" to 16" high. The wooden salad spoons can be purchased at any kitchen supply store.

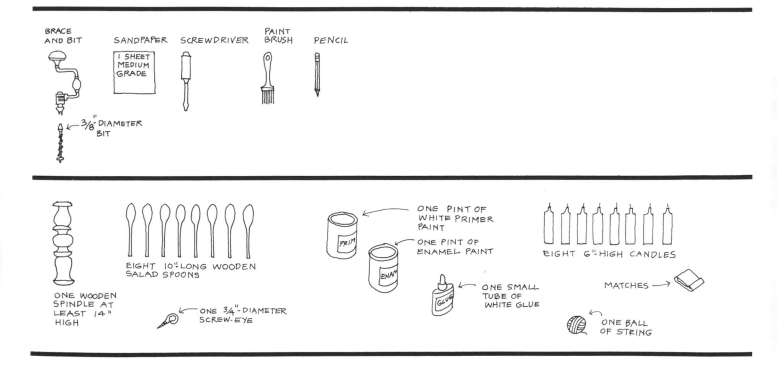

BRACE AND BIT

SANDPAPER — I SHEET MEDIUM GRADE

SCREWDRIVER

PAINT BRUSH

PENCIL

3/8" DIAMETER BIT

ONE WOODEN SPINDLE AT LEAST 14" HIGH

EIGHT 10" LONG WOODEN SALAD SPOONS

ONE 3/4"-DIAMETER SCREW-EYE

ONE PINT OF WHITE PRIMER PAINT

ONE PINT OF ENAMEL PAINT

ONE SMALL TUBE OF WHITE GLUE

EIGHT 6" HIGH CANDLES

MATCHES →

ONE BALL OF STRING

Jess showing the wooden spindle to Adam.

Drilling the Parts

The most important part of this project is drilling the holes at the center of the spindle. They must be drilled straight, or the spoons will hang crookedly and your chandelier won't look as good as you'd like. Try to get a friend to help align the drill so that your holes are straight, as Adam and Jess are doing in the photograph on the facing page.

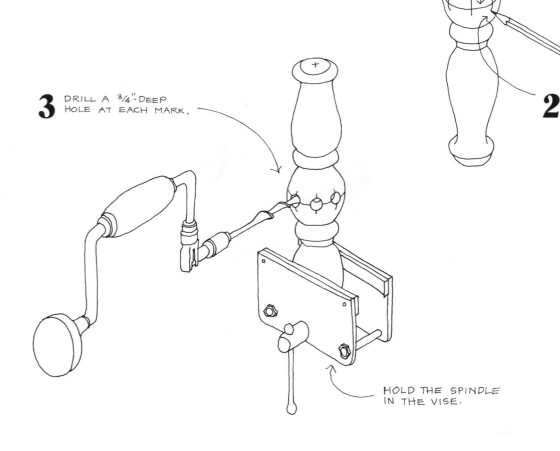

1 DRAW A CIRCLE AROUND THE CENTER OF THE MIDDLE OF THE SPINDLE.

2 MAKE EIGHT EQUALLY SPACED MARKS AROUND THE LINE (ABOUT 1" APART).

3 DRILL A 3/4"-DEEP HOLE AT EACH MARK.

HOLD THE SPINDLE IN THE VISE.

Adam making sure the drill is straight. Jess drilling the holes.

Painting

Using the 1″ brush, carefully paint the sanded spindle with primer paint, making sure no paint gets in the drilled holes. If it does, wipe it out before it dries, or it may prevent the spoon handles from fitting properly. Sand the primed spindle, and again use the 1″ brush to paint the finish coat. Take care as you paint — cover the table with newspaper, and try not to spill the paint. Remember, you're teaching yourself the art of carpentry. Set up properly and have patience. Clean your brush after each use so you can use it again on other projects.

5 WHEN THE PRIMER PAINT HAS DRIED, SAND LIGHTLY AGAIN, THEN CLEAN AND PAINT WITH ONE THICK COAT OF ENAMEL. ALLOW IT TO DRY OVERNIGHT.

4 SAND THE SPINDLE LIGHTLY AND PAINT IT WITH ONE COAT OF WHITE PRIMER PAINT.

DON'T GET ANY PAINT IN THE HOLES BECAUSE THE SPOONS WON'T FIT.

6 CURL A PIECE OF SANDPAPER AND SAND THE SPOON HANDLES UNTIL THEY FIT INTO THE 3/8″ DIAMETER HOLES.

Jess putting the finish coat of enamel on the primed and sanded spindle.

Assembling the Parts

Assembling the candle chandelier parts is very easy. The eight spoons are glued into their holes, the screw-eye is twisted into the spindle with a screwdriver, and the candles are attached to the spoons with melted wax. The candle chandelier is then ready for hanging in a special place, using string attached to the screw-eye.

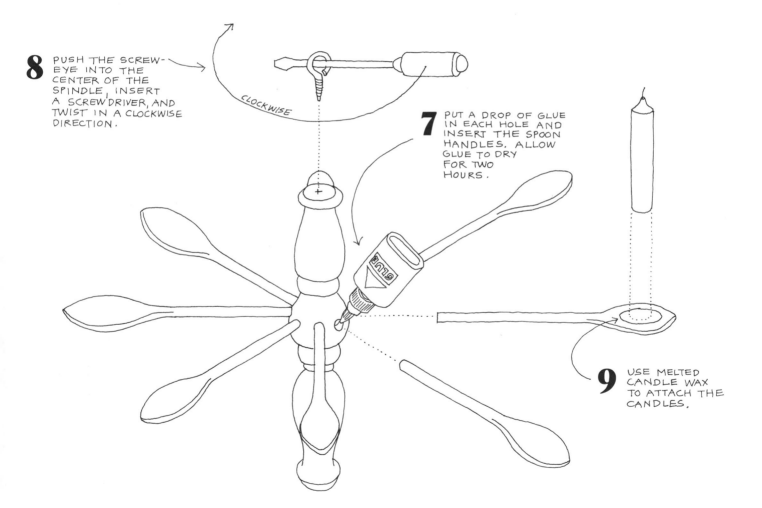

8 PUSH THE SCREW-EYE INTO THE CENTER OF THE SPINDLE, INSERT A SCREWDRIVER, AND TWIST IN A CLOCKWISE DIRECTION.

CLOCKWISE

7 PUT A DROP OF GLUE IN EACH HOLE AND INSERT THE SPOON HANDLES. ALLOW GLUE TO DRY FOR TWO HOURS.

GLUE

9 USE MELTED CANDLE WAX TO ATTACH THE CANDLES.

108

Jess gluing the spoons into their holes in the painted spindle.

Party Time

Now all you've got to do is figure out a reason for a party, especially one at night so the candlelight can create the perfect atmosphere. Again, be really careful with matches.

The group celebrates with a cake.

Weekend Projects

Weekend Projects

If you've built one or more of the one-day projects, you're ready to move on to the more difficult and more time-consuming weekend projects.

Become familiar with each weekend project — all of which are pictured on the facing page — by reading pages 114 to 155. This will help you choose a project that you like and that you're sure you have the ability to build. If you work with friends, you should be able to build more than one project during a weekend, but don't rush — you must always be patient and try to do your best work.

On the following pages, each project is arranged in order of difficulty: doll cradle, stilts, puppet theater, and easel. If you choose the easel, you'll be choosing the most difficult project, but have confidence and follow the step-by-step directions, and you should have no problems.

Doll Cradle

Puppet Theater

Stilts

Easel

Doll Cradle

The doll cradle is one of the most beautiful projects in this book. It's both old-fashioned and modern at the same time — a clean, simple design made from natural pine, sanded to a smooth finish. It makes a great gift or a lovely bed to gently rock your doll to sleep.

Our doll cradle is designed to develop skills with all the important tools — both types of saws, brace and bit, and hammer. It'll be a test of your sanding ability.

Since it's made from pine boards, it gets more attractive with each sanding.

Read the instructions thoroughly before you begin. You'll want to have a full understanding of the project as you work.

Assembling the Tools and Materials

Below is a list of the tools and materials you'll need to build the doll cradle. It's very, very important that the 6'-length of 1x10 pine not be warped (curved) so that your finished cradle won't be crooked. Make sure you inform the people at your lumberyard about this.

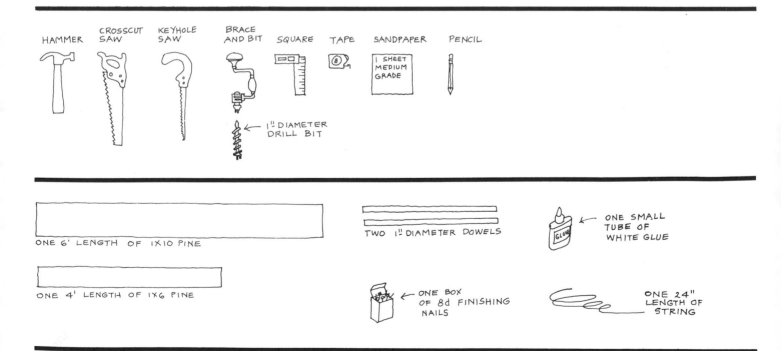

HAMMER   CROSSCUT SAW   KEYHOLE SAW   BRACE AND BIT   SQUARE   TAPE   SANDPAPER | 1 SHEET MEDIUM GRADE   PENCIL

1" DIAMETER DRILL BIT

ONE 6' LENGTH OF 1X10 PINE

ONE 4' LENGTH OF 1X6 PINE

TWO 1" DIAMETER DOWELS

ONE SMALL TUBE OF WHITE GLUE

ONE BOX OF 8d FINISHING NAILS

ONE 24" LENGTH OF STRING

Molly getting ready the tools and materials to build the doll cradle.

Sawing the Parts

Below are the five steps for laying out and sawing the wooden parts needed to build your doll cradle. It's important to make straight and true saw cuts so that the cradle will fit together properly. Take your time when sawing, and, if possible, have a friend watch to make sure you're sawing along the line.

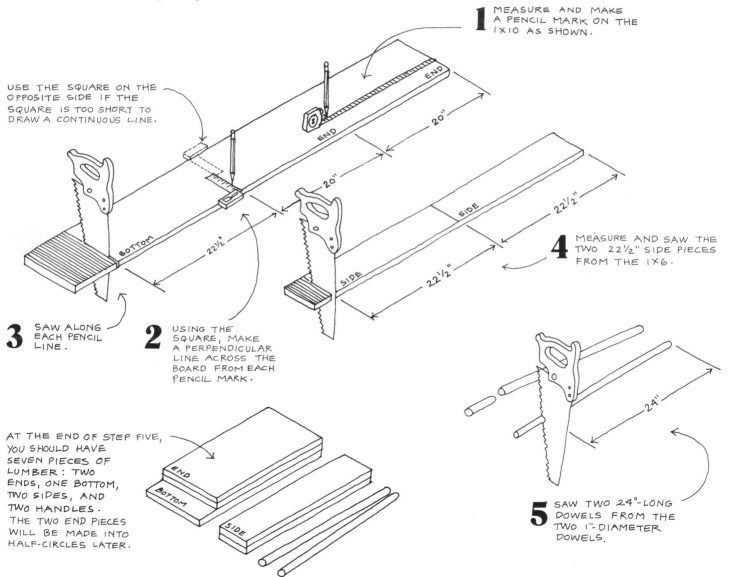

1 MEASURE AND MAKE A PENCIL MARK ON THE 1X10 AS SHOWN.

USE THE SQUARE ON THE OPPOSITE SIDE IF THE SQUARE IS TOO SHORT TO DRAW A CONTINUOUS LINE.

4 MEASURE AND SAW THE TWO 22½" SIDE PIECES FROM THE 1X6.

3 SAW ALONG EACH PENCIL LINE.

2 USING THE SQUARE, MAKE A PERPENDICULAR LINE ACROSS THE BOARD FROM EACH PENCIL MARK.

AT THE END OF STEP FIVE, YOU SHOULD HAVE SEVEN PIECES OF LUMBER: TWO ENDS, ONE BOTTOM, TWO SIDES, AND TWO HANDLES. THE TWO END PIECES WILL BE MADE INTO HALF-CIRCLES LATER.

5 SAW TWO 24"-LONG DOWELS FROM THE TWO 1"-DIAMETER DOWELS.

Laying Out the Half-Circles

The three steps below show you how to draw the cradle's two half-circle end pieces with a string compass. After the compass is tied to the nail at one end and a pencil at the other, its radius (string length) should be 9". Check this with your tape before drawing your half circles.

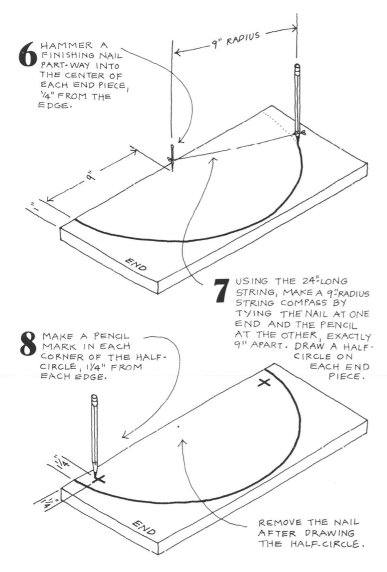

6 HAMMER A FINISHING NAIL PART-WAY INTO THE CENTER OF EACH END PIECE, 1/4" FROM THE EDGE.

9" RADIUS

9"

END

7 USING THE 24"-LONG STRING, MAKE A 9"-RADIUS STRING COMPASS BY TYING THE NAIL AT ONE END AND THE PENCIL AT THE OTHER, EXACTLY 9" APART. DRAW A HALF-CIRCLE ON EACH END PIECE.

8 MAKE A PENCIL MARK IN EACH CORNER OF THE HALF-CIRCLE, 1/4" FROM EACH EDGE.

1/4"

1/4"

END

REMOVE THE NAIL AFTER DRAWING THE HALF-CIRCLE.

Molly drawing the half-circles on the end pieces.

Sawing the Half-Circles

Below are the directions to finish the two end pieces. Remember to turn the wood around when the point of the bit pierces the wood, and then drill from the other side to get a perfect hole. This procedure is described on page 32. Keep the keyhole saw on the line as you cut the half-circle. You'll want your cradle to rock smoothly.

10 DRILL HOLES AT EACH CROSS-MARK IN THE CORNER OF EACH HALF-CIRCLE WITH THE 1"-DIAMETER DRILL BIT.

9 USING THE KEYHOLE SAW, CUT ALONG THE HALF-CIRCLE LINE. DURING CUTTING, CHANGE THE POSITION OF THE WOOD PERIODICALLY SO THAT THE KEYHOLE SAWING IS COMFORTABLE. SEE THE PHOTOGRAPH ON THE FACING PAGE.

HOLD YOUR WORK STEADY IN THE VISE.

END

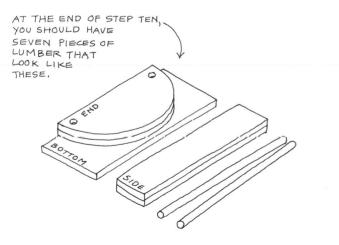

AT THE END OF STEP TEN, YOU SHOULD HAVE SEVEN PIECES OF LUMBER THAT LOOK LIKE THESE.

END

BOTTOM

SIDE

Molly keyhole-sawing the ends, and Jess cutting the sides.

Assembling the Parts

Before you begin to assemble your doll cradle, make sure that all the wooden parts are sanded until they are smooth and without rough edges. After you have it built, carefully sand it again, using a sanding block such as the one described on page 40.

Steps ten through fourteen show how to assemble the doll cradle. It's best to have a friend steady the wood pieces as you nail them in place.

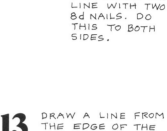

14 NAIL THE INSIDE EDGE OF THE SIDE ALONG THE LINE WITH TWO 8d NAILS. DO THIS TO BOTH SIDES.

13 DRAW A LINE FROM THE EDGE OF THE BOTTOM TO THE CENTER OF THE HOLE.

12 PLACE THE TOP EDGE OF THE BOTTOM PIECE ALONG THE LINE AND NAIL IT INTO PLACE WITH THREE 8d NAILS. TURN THE ASSEMBLY OVER AND DO THE SAME THING TO THE OTHER END.

11 DRAW A PARALLEL LINE 6¾" FROM THE EDGE OF EACH END PIECE.

15 GLUE THE DOWELS IN THEIR HOLES.

Jess nailing the ends to the bottom and Molly steadying the work.

Jess nailing the ends to the sides. Molly getting the dowel handles ready.

Bedtime

After your cradle is finished, you're ready to play with it. You'll need small baby blankets, a pillow, and, of course, your favorite doll. Our cradle is designed for dolls that are 16" to 18" long (average doll) but will accomodate dolls up to 22" long.

Whether you've made the doll cradle for a gift or for yourself, it'll provide a nice, secure place for any doll. Have fun.

Molly rocking her doll to sleep.

Stilts

Stilts are one of the most exciting projects you can build. They're easy to make and can make you feel ten-feet tall after you've practiced with them for a while. It's always fun to look in windows or get to high spots such as trees, rooftops, shelves — even cookie jars — that you couldn't normally reach. Best of all, it's fun to feel like a giant.

Our stilts are designed to improve your drilling abilities and introduce you to nuts-and-bolts type hardware.

The wing nut is used because you don't need a wrench or pliers to tighten it — just twist with your fingers, and it's tight.

Assembling the Tools and Materials

Below is a list of tools and materials needed to make stilts. The stilt poles are made from pine baluster stock trim, and the steps are made from 5/4x4 lumber. Thinner lumber is too weak, so make sure you order the proper materials.

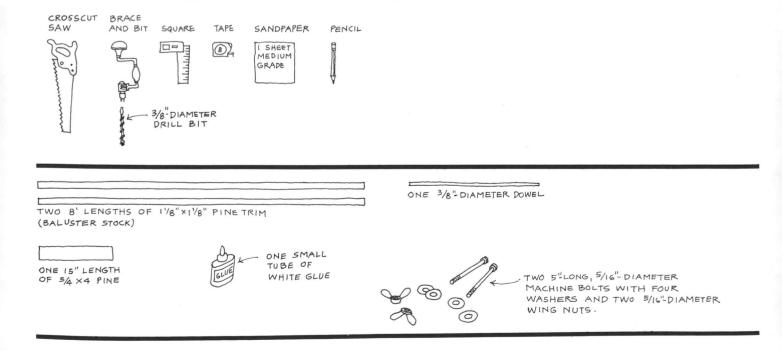

Ben getting the materials ready, and Adam and Jess checking the tools.

Making the Poles

Below are the four steps to making your stilt poles. First, you must saw two 7'-long poles, then drill the holes in them to hold the steps. Read page 32 again to refresh your memory on the use of the brace and bit. Remember, to get clean, splinterless holes you must drill through the wood until the point of the drill has pierced the other side. Then turn the wood over, use the small pierced hole to start the drill again, and finish drilling the hole. You've got sixteen holes to drill, and they must be clean, so do your best work.

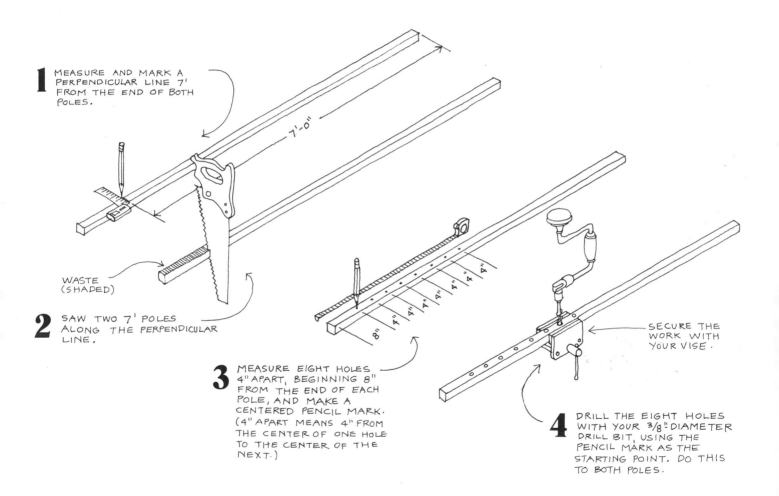

1 MEASURE AND MARK A PERPENDICULAR LINE 7' FROM THE END OF BOTH POLES.

7'-0"

WASTE (SHADED)

2 SAW TWO 7' POLES ALONG THE PERPENDICULAR LINE.

3 MEASURE EIGHT HOLES 4" APART, BEGINNING 8" FROM THE END OF EACH POLE, AND MAKE A CENTERED PENCIL MARK. (4" APART MEANS 4" FROM THE CENTER OF ONE HOLE TO THE CENTER OF THE NEXT.)

8" 4" 4" 4" 4" 4" 4" 4"

SECURE THE WORK WITH YOUR VISE.

4 DRILL THE EIGHT HOLES WITH YOUR 3/8" DIAMETER DRILL BIT, USING THE PENCIL MARK AS THE STARTING POINT. DO THIS TO BOTH POLES.

Jess drilling the poles, and Adam starting to saw the stilt steps.

Making the Steps

Making the stilt steps is a little tricky because they're so small. Use the vise to steady your work and saw very, very carefully. As you drill the hole in step seven, be very sure it's straight. It's a 3½"-deep hole, so if it's off slightly, it'll be crooked, and your stilts won't work as well as you'd like. Sand all parts before gluing.

9 SAW TWO 2"-LONG PEGS FROM THE 3/8" DIAMETER WOOD DOWEL.

5 USING THE SQUARE AS A STRAIGHTEDGE, MEASURE AND DRAW THE TWO STILT STEPS ON THE 15"-LONG 5/4 X 4 PIECE OF PINE.

6 SAW THE STEPS ALONG THE LINES YOU DREW IN STEP FIVE.

WASTE (SHADED)

7 DRILL A 3/8"-DIAMETER HOLE COMPLETELY THROUGH THE WOODEN STEP, 3/4" FROM THE EDGE. HAVE A FRIEND MAKE VERY SURE YOU ARE DRILLING STRAIGHT.

8 DRILL A 3/8"-DIAMETER HOLE 1" DEEP INTO THE WOOD, WITH ITS CENTER EXACTLY 4" FROM THE HOLE IN STEP SEVEN.

USE THE VISE TO HOLD YOUR WORK.

10 GLUE THE 2"-LONG PEGS INTO THE LOWER HOLE OF EACH STEP.

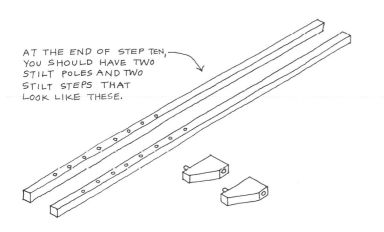

AT THE END OF STEP TEN, YOU SHOULD HAVE TWO STILT POLES AND TWO STILT STEPS THAT LOOK LIKE THESE.

Adam gluing the pegs into the stilt steps.

Finishing the Job

To finish your stilts, choose the height you want to be when you use them, then attach the steps to the poles according to the diagram below. It's best to start at a lower level, then you can raise the steps as you get used to walking higher.

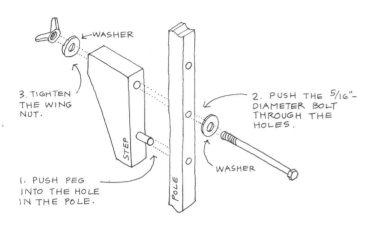

WASHER

3. TIGHTEN THE WING NUT.

2. PUSH THE 5/16"-DIAMETER BOLT THROUGH THE HOLES.

WASHER

STEP

POLE

1. PUSH PEG INTO THE HOLE IN THE POLE.

Ben and Jess attaching the stilt steps to the poles.

Ben's first time on the stilts.

Puppet Theater

This puppet theater is designed to make your puppet shows bright and exciting. It has a classical facade, painted your favorite color, with an arched stage area and two curtains. It's a great deal of work, but you'll be more than pleased after you've finished and set up your first show.

The puppet theater project is designed to continue your development as a carpenter by using all the major tools. All the tasks are simple, however, and if

you follow the step-by-step directions, you should have no problems. Work carefully. Care about your craft.

Assembling the Tools and Materials

Below is a list of tools and materials needed to build your puppet theater. The 20"x30" sheet of ¼"-thick plywood is a standard size often sold in home-supply centers. If you can't find that size, you may have to

buy a 24"x48" sheet and either have the lumberyard cut it to the 20"x30" size or saw it, with your crosscut saw, by yourself.

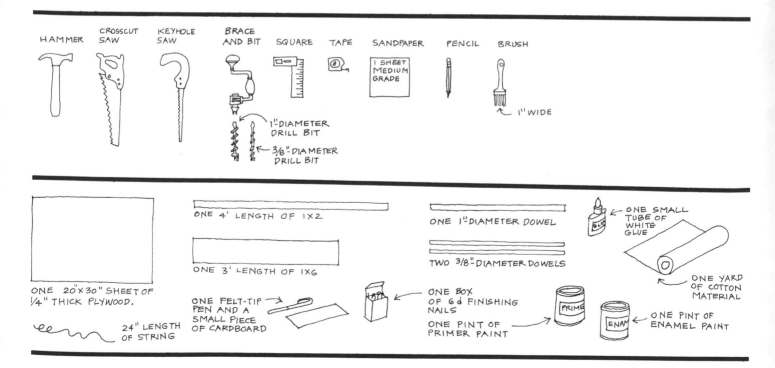

Adam laying out the materials, and Ben and Jess checking the tools.

Sawing the Parts

Below are the five steps to saw all but one of the wooden parts needed to build your puppet theater; how to saw the front is shown on the next two pages. Don't hesitate to use the vise to steady your work if you find it's necessary. You'll want to make straight saw cuts so your project will fit together perfectly.

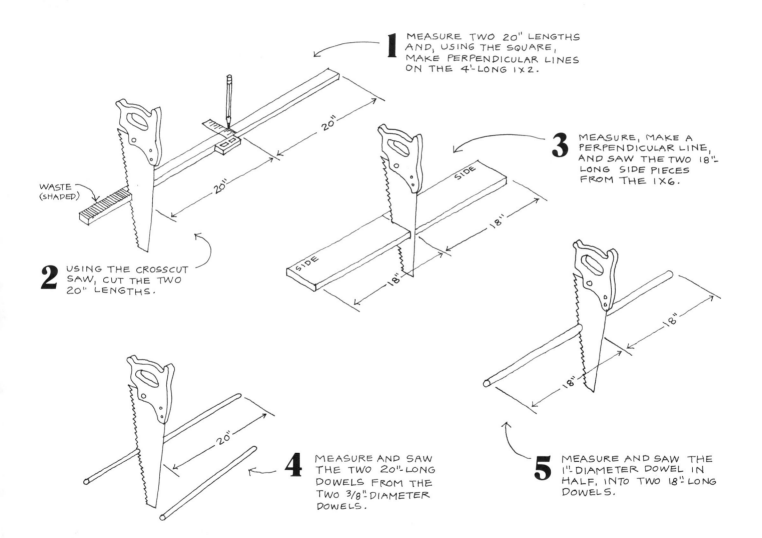

1 MEASURE TWO 20" LENGTHS AND, USING THE SQUARE, MAKE PERPENDICULAR LINES ON THE 4'-LONG 1x2.

WASTE (SHADED)

2 USING THE CROSSCUT SAW, CUT THE TWO 20" LENGTHS.

3 MEASURE, MAKE A PERPENDICULAR LINE, AND SAW THE TWO 18"-LONG SIDE PIECES FROM THE 1x6.

4 MEASURE AND SAW THE TWO 20"-LONG DOWELS FROM THE TWO 3/8"-DIAMETER DOWELS.

5 MEASURE AND SAW THE 1"-DIAMETER DOWEL IN HALF, INTO TWO 18"-LONG DOWELS.

Laying Out the Front

Lay out the theater front according to the directions below. Use a straight piece of narrow lumber to connect your pencil marks to draw a long straight line. The string compass is explained in greater detail on page 119.

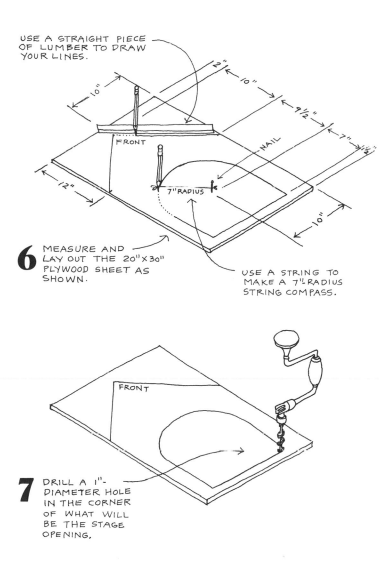

USE A STRAIGHT PIECE OF LUMBER TO DRAW YOUR LINES.

FRONT

2"

10"

9½"

7"

1¾"

NAIL

7" RADIUS

10"

12"

10"

6 MEASURE AND LAY OUT THE 20"×30" PLYWOOD SHEET AS SHOWN.

USE A STRING TO MAKE A 7" RADIUS STRING COMPASS.

FRONT

7 DRILL A 1"-DIAMETER HOLE IN THE CORNER OF WHAT WILL BE THE STAGE OPENING.

Adam drawing the half-circle with the string compass.

Sawing the Front

Sawing the puppet theater front piece is fun because the ¼" plywood is very easy to cut, so the work goes fast. But you must be careful that the saw blade, especially on the keyhole saw, does not stray from the line that you've drawn. Take your time to cut a perfect circle.

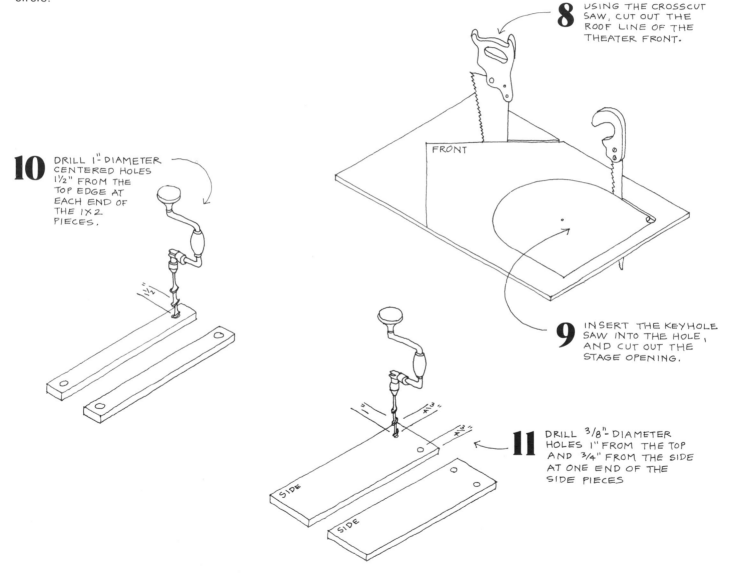

8 USING THE CROSSCUT SAW, CUT OUT THE ROOF LINE OF THE THEATER FRONT.

10 DRILL 1"-DIAMETER CENTERED HOLES 1½" FROM THE TOP EDGE AT EACH END OF THE 1×2 PIECES.

9 INSERT THE KEYHOLE SAW INTO THE HOLE, AND CUT OUT THE STAGE OPENING.

11 DRILL ³/₈"-DIAMETER HOLES 1" FROM THE TOP AND ¾" FROM THE SIDE AT ONE END OF THE SIDE PIECES

Carefully sand all your wooden pieces, making sure there are no rough edges. Check to see if the dowels fit into the holes you've drilled into the 1x2s and the side pieces — 1" dowels into the 1"-diameter holes and ⅜" dowels into the ⅜"-diameter holes. If they're too tight, sand them until they fit properly.

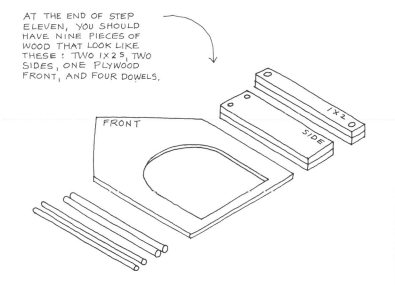

AT THE END OF STEP ELEVEN, YOU SHOULD HAVE NINE PIECES OF WOOD THAT LOOK LIKE THESE : TWO 1X2S, TWO SIDES, ONE PLYWOOD FRONT, AND FOUR DOWELS.

FRONT

1X2

SIDE

Adam keyhole-sawing the front piece.

Assembling the Parts

Assembling the parts of the puppet theater is easy if you follow the four steps below and you drive your nails straight. If a nail starts going crooked, pull it out and start another one in a different spot. The nails must be straight for the puppet theater to be strong.

13 NAIL THE 1X2S TO THE 1"-DIAMETER DOWELS (AFTER INSERTING THE DOWELS INTO THE HOLES) WITH 6d FINISHING NAILS TO MAKE A FRAME FOR THE STAGE.

1X2

1X2

12 NAIL THE FRONT TO THE SIDES WITH THE 6d FINISHING NAILS.

FRONT

SIDE

SIDE

BEFORE NAILING, MAKE SURE THE HOLES OF THE SIDES ARE AT THE TOP.

FRONT

MAKE A SIGN WITH CARDBOARD AND YOUR FELT-TIP PEN, AND GLUE IT ONTO THE FRAME.

THEATER

14 PAINT THE FRONT AND SIDE UNIT WITH WHITE PRIMER, THEN ENAMEL OF A COLOR OF YOUR CHOICE.

ENAMEL

PRIMER

FRAME

15 AFTER THE PAINT DRIES, NAIL, FROM THE REAR, THE FRAME TO THE FRONT PIECE WITH 6d FINISHING NAILS.

Ben assembling the frame, and Jess painting the front unit.

Hanging the Curtains

Making and hanging the curtains in your puppet theater is a very simple job. Just cut out each curtain, fold over and staple a loop as shown in step seventeen (if you can sew, you may prefer to stitch the loop), then hang the curtains on dowels as shown in step eighteen. If you have different kinds of material available, you may want to make the front curtains different from the backdrop.

17 FOLD OVER 2" ALONG THE TOP OF EACH CURTAIN AND STAPLE IT TO MAKE A "LOOP."

16 MEASURE AND CUT TWO 12" X 20" STAGE FRONT CURTAINS AND ONE 24"X20" BACKDROP CURTAIN FROM THE YARD OF COTTON MATERIAL.

SPREAD APART FRONT CURTAINS TO OPEN THEM.

18 PUSH THE 3/8"- DIAMETER DOWELS THROUGH THE HOLES IN THE SIDES AND THE LOOPS IN THE CURTAINS. THE CURTAINS WILL "RIDE" ALONG THE DOWELS.

Jess tapping the dowels into place while Molly steadies the theater.

Show Time

Now that you've finished your puppet theater, it's time to round up all your friends and their puppets and put on a big show. They'll be amazed that you made the theater by yourself. And you, of course, should be proud.

AND YOU THOUGHT IT WAS JUST FOR HAND PUPPETS, DIDN'T YOU?

Molly and Jess practicing their puppet play.

Easel

The easel is an upright frame that holds your painting or sketchpad as you paint or draw while standing. It's a necessary tool for any artist and works indoors or out. If you're artistically inclined, you'll find that the easel will be a big help with your artwork.

Our easel is very easy to build, and none of the tasks are very time-consuming. Remember, though, to be patient and work carefully. Carpentry is really an art form, and you'll want your easel to be a work of art.

Assembling the Tools and Materials

Below is a list of tools and materials needed to build your easel. Some home centers or lumberyards don't stock the 24"x24" plywood size. You may have to buy a 24"x48" piece and have it cut to size (in half), or you may have to cut it yourself (with a crosscut saw).

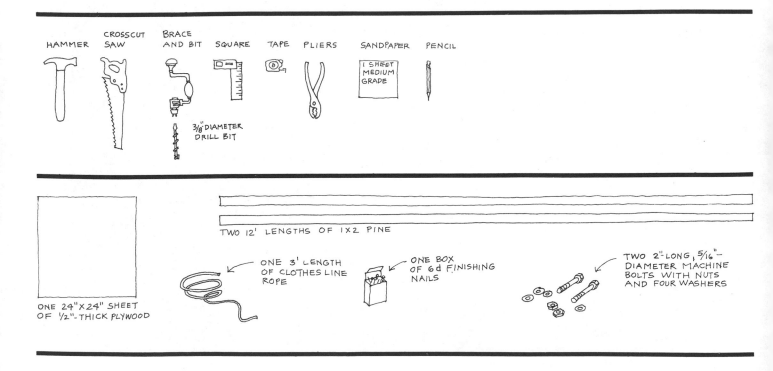

Adam, Jess, and Ben setting up the materials, while Molly checks the tools.

Sawing the Parts

Below are the instructions for sawing and drilling the four legs and sawing the back and ledge pieces. Take care to saw and drill straight and true. Remember, you're making a piece of furniture.

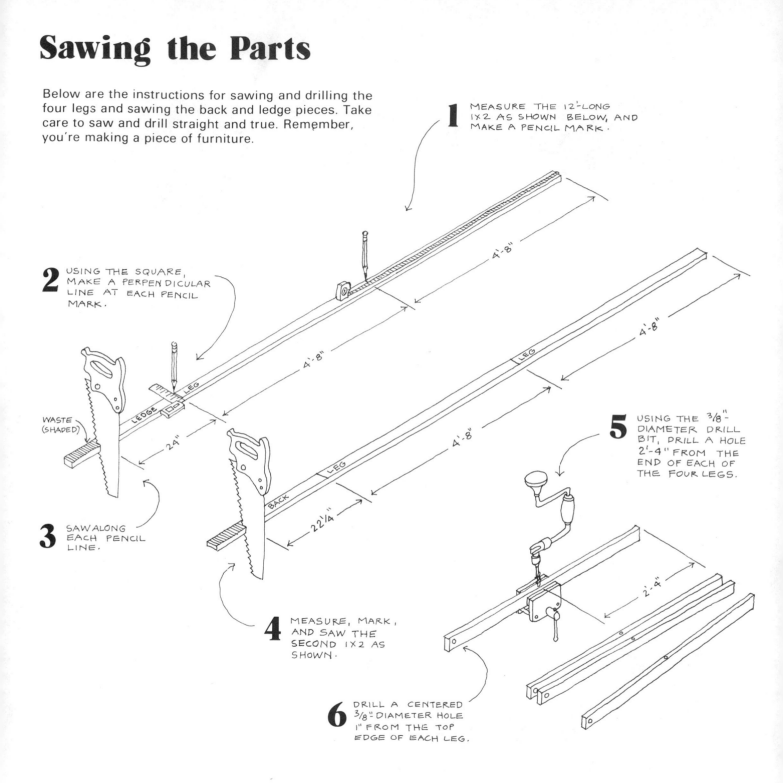

1 MEASURE THE 12'-LONG 1X2 AS SHOWN BELOW, AND MAKE A PENCIL MARK.

2 USING THE SQUARE, MAKE A PERPENDICULAR LINE AT EACH PENCIL MARK.

WASTE (SHADED)

3 SAW ALONG EACH PENCIL LINE.

LEDGE

LEG

24"

4'-8"

4'-8"

4'-8"

LEG

BACK

22¼"

4 MEASURE, MARK, AND SAW THE SECOND 1X2 AS SHOWN.

5 USING THE 3/8"-DIAMETER DRILL BIT, DRILL A HOLE 2'-4" FROM THE END OF EACH OF THE FOUR LEGS.

2'-4"

6 DRILL A CENTERED 3/8" DIAMETER HOLE 1" FROM THE TOP EDGE OF EACH LEG.

Jess making sure that Adam drills a straight hole, while Molly steadies the 1x2 lumber for Ben to saw.

Making the Front and Back

The front assembly consists of the drawing board, with the ledge, nailed to two legs. The back assembly consists of a back piece nailed to two legs. Instructions for making them are shown below. The back will be very wobbly until you attach it to the front, as shown in step eleven on page 152, so be careful with it.

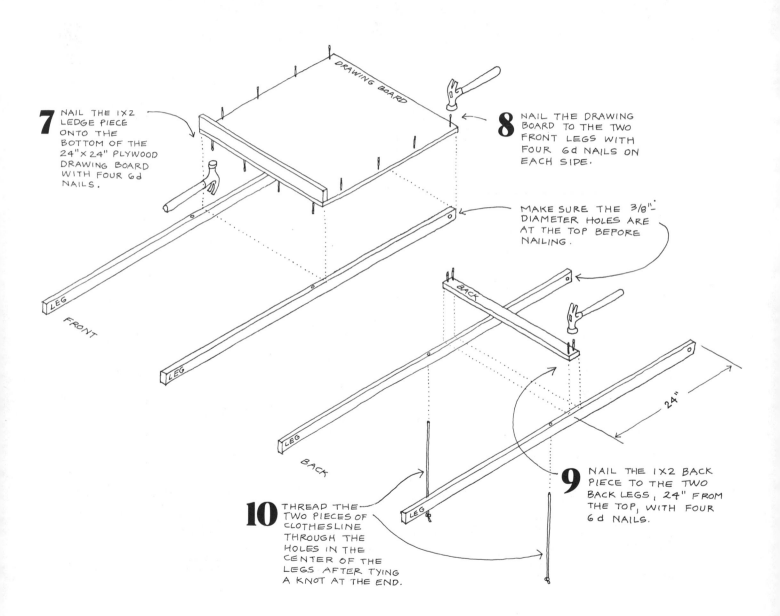

7 NAIL THE 1X2 LEDGE PIECE ONTO THE BOTTOM OF THE 24"X 24" PLYWOOD DRAWING BOARD WITH FOUR 6d NAILS.

8 NAIL THE DRAWING BOARD TO THE TWO FRONT LEGS WITH FOUR 6d NAILS ON EACH SIDE.

DRAWING BOARD

LEG

FRONT

LEG

MAKE SURE THE 3/8"-DIAMETER HOLES ARE AT THE TOP BEFORE NAILING.

BACK

LEG

BACK

24"

10 THREAD THE TWO PIECES OF CLOTHESLINE THROUGH THE HOLES IN THE CENTER OF THE LEGS AFTER TYING A KNOT AT THE END.

9 NAIL THE 1X2 BACK PIECE TO THE TWO BACK LEGS, 24" FROM THE TOP, WITH FOUR 6d NAILS.

Jess nailing the ledge to the drawing board, while Molly threads the clothesline through the holes.

Assembling the Parts

Here are the three steps to finish your easel. Make sure all the parts are sanded and well-built before you begin.

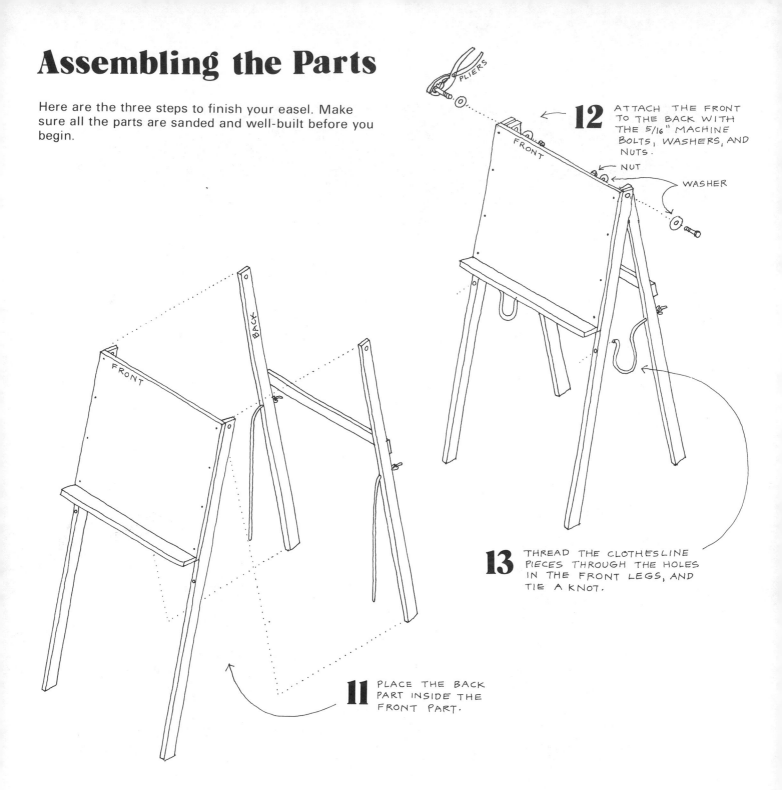

12 ATTACH THE FRONT TO THE BACK WITH THE 5/16" MACHINE BOLTS, WASHERS, AND NUTS.

NUT

WASHER

PLIERS

FRONT

BACK

FRONT

13 THREAD THE CLOTHESLINE PIECES THROUGH THE HOLES IN THE FRONT LEGS, AND TIE A KNOT.

11 PLACE THE BACK PART INSIDE THE FRONT PART.

Molly, Jess, and Adam attaching the front and back easel parts with nuts and bolts.

Figure Drawing

Your easel is lightweight so you can carry it to where you want to paint or draw. It will hold canvases or drawing pads by simply resting them on the ledge. Paper or thin cardboard should be taped or tacked to the drawing-board surface. The ledge will also hold your paints, markers, pencils, or whatever you're using to do your artwork. The easel folds flat for storage.

If you're artistically inclined, your easel will be a most helpful piece of furniture. If you take care of it, it should last a long, long time.

IT FOLDS FLAT SO YOU CAN CARRY IT TO WHERE YOU WANT TO WORK.

Adam using Jess, Molly, and Ben as models.

One-Week Projects

One-Week Projects

If you've built one or more of the weekend projects, you're ready to make one of the more elaborate, time-consuming one-week projects.

Choose one of the three projects shown on the next page after you've become familiar with the instructions for each. Get a cost estimate for materials from your local home-center or lumberyard, and make sure you have the necessary tools. Of course, if you plan to build the raft, you'll need a body of water; the lemonade stand, a place where people gather; and the coaster car, a safe, paved hill. It's best to work with friends on projects of this size and complexity, and it's more fun to share the thrill of the finished project.

Each project is arranged in order of difficulty: raft, lemonade stand, and coaster car. If you choose the coaster car, you'll be building the most difficult project in the book, but if you take your time and carefully follow each step, you should have no problems.

Raft

Lemonade Stand

Coaster Car

159

Raft

This raft is designed to be a floating surface that can be used as a boat, a diving platform, or just a place to fish or on which to lie and get tanned. Building the raft is very heavy work, so you'll need a few friends to help you, just as Huckleberry Finn needed Tom Sawyer.

The raft is designed to begin your involvement in larger carpentry projects. It has two main parts: the top surface and the floats. Each part must be made separately, then connected together. The concept of different phases in building is common, especially in housebuilding. In this project, the floats might be considered the foundation, and the top surface, the first floor of a house. The raft is built with simple, rough carpentry techniques. It must be strong, so your nailing has to be true, and it must have no rough edges, so sanding is important.

Assembling the Tools and Materials

Below is a list of tools and materials needed to build the raft. You may have to saw and trim your logs to get them to the proper size. If you have trouble finding them, old telegraph poles, railroad ties, or large lumber such as 8x8s are good substitutes. New house construction sites often have logs cut in 5' lengths, after trees have been cut for the driveway or house site. Town dumps often have logs, but you may have to cut them to size. Keep looking — any large piece of wood will do.

HAMMER CROSSCUT SAW SQUARE TAPE SCREWDRIVER SANDPAPER PENCIL

1 SHEET MEDIUM GRADE

ONE 12'-LONG 2x4

EIGHT 8'-LONG 2x4'S

ONE 1" DIAMETER SCREW-EYE

FOUR LOGS AT LEAST 8" DIAMETER AND 5' LONG

TWO BOXES OF 12d COMMON NAILS (YOU'LL NEED ABOUT EIGHTY 12d NAILS.

50' OF ½" DIAMETER ROPE

Jess and Adam unloading the 2x4s from the truck.

Sawing the Raft-Top Parts

Below are the instructions for sawing the 2x4s for the
raft top. Try to make perfect perpendicular saw cuts.
They'll make your raft look better.

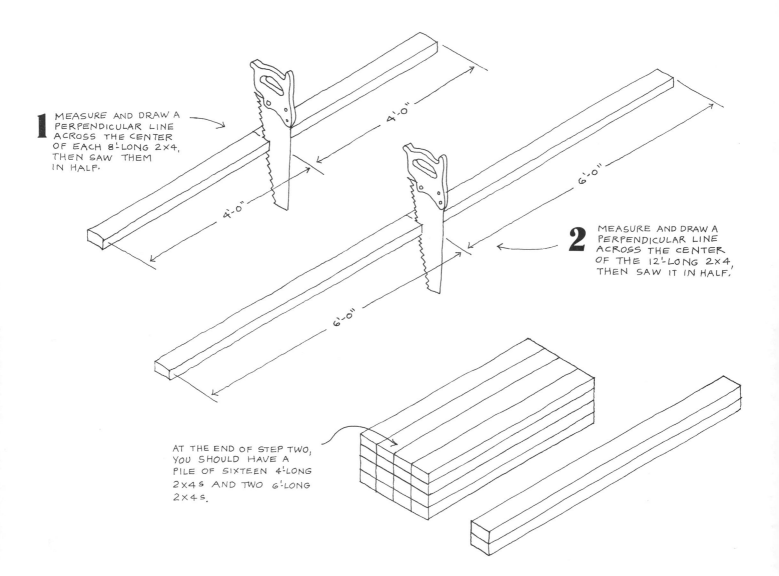

1 MEASURE AND DRAW A
PERPENDICULAR LINE
ACROSS THE CENTER
OF EACH 8'-LONG 2x4,
THEN SAW THEM
IN HALF.

4'-0"

4'-0"

6'-0"

2 MEASURE AND DRAW A
PERPENDICULAR LINE
ACROSS THE CENTER
OF THE 12'-LONG 2x4,
THEN SAW IT IN HALF.

6'-0"

AT THE END OF STEP TWO,
YOU SHOULD HAVE A
PILE OF SIXTEEN 4'-LONG
2x4s AND TWO 6'-LONG
2x4s.

Adam measuring, Ben steadying, Molly sawing, and Jess stacking the 2x4s.

Assembling the Raft-Top Parts

You must be careful in nailing the raft-top parts together. Each nail must be straight and true for the raft to be strong. If a nail starts going crooked, pull it out and start hammering another in a different spot. After your raft top is assembled, sand all the rough edges so they don't scrape your skin when you're swimming.

3 MEASURE AND MAKE A PENCIL MARK EVERY 4" ALONG THE EDGE OF EACH 6'-LONG 2×4.

4 USING TWO 12d NAILS AT EACH END, NAIL THE 4'-LONG 2×4S ON-TO THE PENCIL MARKS ON EACH 6'-LONG 2×4. THE 2×4S ARE REALLY 3½" WIDE, SO THERE WILL BE A ½" GAP BETWEEN THEM FOR WATER TO ESCAPE.

Molly and Ben nailing the raft-top parts together.

Trimming the Logs

You probably won't be lucky enough to find four 8"-diameter logs that are 5' long. You'll probably have to saw your logs to size from a fallen tree or larger logs. This'll be the most difficult task of the project. The work will seem endless, but you'll feel very proud when you've completed it, so have patience and work hard.

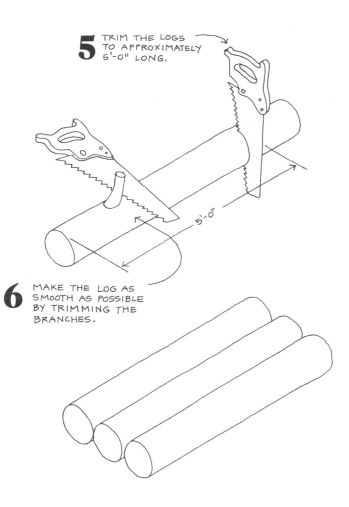

5 TRIM THE LOGS TO APPROXIMATELY 5'-0" LONG.

5'-0"

6 MAKE THE LOG AS SMOOTH AS POSSIBLE BY TRIMMING THE BRANCHES.

Making the Floats

You'll need two floats, one for each side of your raft. Each float is made from two logs tied together, as shown below. Have a friend hold the logs steady (in shallow water) while you wrap the rope around them. Tie your knots tightly to make sure they won't unravel.

7 FLOAT TWO OF THE LOGS IN SHALLOW WATER, AND TIE THEM TOGETHER TWICE AT EACH END WITH THE ½"-DIAMETER ROPE WRAPPED IN A FIGURE-EIGHT AROUND THE LOGS.

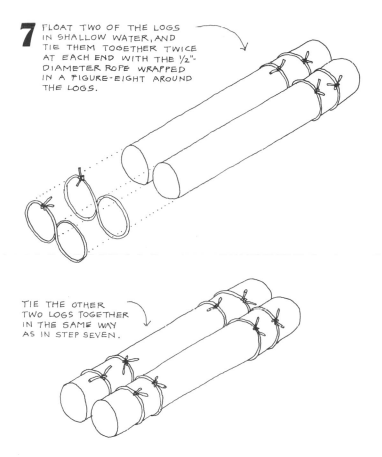

TIE THE OTHER TWO LOGS TOGETHER IN THE SAME WAY AS IN STEP SEVEN.

Ben steadying the logs while Adam ties them with a figure-eight.

Finishing the Job

In shallow water, have friends help you lift the raft top onto the floats. Slide the floats to each end of the raft top, then nail at least three 12d nails through the sides of the raft top, angled down into the floats. After you've attached the screw eye, you'll have a way to tie the raft to a tree or a post on shore.

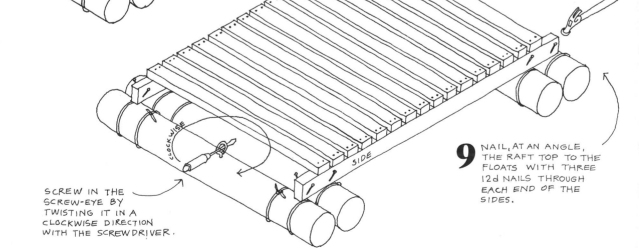

8 LIFT THE RAFT TOP ONTO THE FLOATS. POSITION THEM UNDER EACH END OF THE RAFT TOP.

9 NAIL, AT AN ANGLE, THE RAFT TOP TO THE FLOATS WITH THREE 12d NAILS THROUGH EACH END OF THE SIDES.

SCREW IN THE SCREW-EYE BY TWISTING IT IN A CLOCKWISE DIRECTION WITH THE SCREWDRIVER.

168

Jess nailing the raft top to the floats. Ben and Adam holding the work steady.

Launching

Since you've built most of the raft in the water, once you've hammered in the last nail attaching the raft top to the floats, your raft is already launched. It makes a great diving, fishing, and sunning platform, but, best of all, it's a boat; it goes with the current and can be guided with a long pole, which you can make by trimming a sapling.

Be sure to tie the raft to a tree or post on shore, or bring it onto shore, after you've finished using it. You don't want it to float away when you're not looking.

Molly getting sun, while Jess guides the raft with a pole.

Lemonade Stand

This lemonade stand is designed to be a perfect little store to sell lemonade: bright yellow to attract patrons, a big shelf to make lemonade, and signs to give price information. It's rather large and weighs forty-five pounds, but it's not difficult to build, and if you enjoy selling lemonade, it could pay for itself in a few weekends.

The lemonade stand is designed to introduce you to plywood and its ability to make big, furniturelike projects in a short time. You'll have to drive your nails straight and true and sand well before painting. You'll also be able to try your hand at sign-painting.

Assembling the Tools and Materials

Below is a list of tools and materials needed to build your lemonade stand. It's important to keep your plastic sheet over the plywood until it's painted, or it'll warp and become unusable.

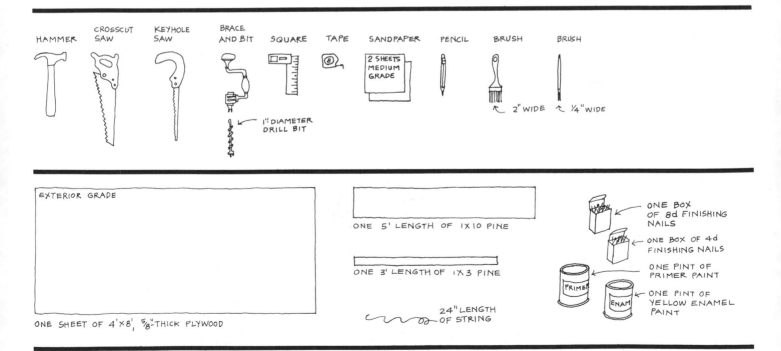

Molly and Ben unloading the materials.

Laying Out the Front

Lay out the lemonade stand front according to the directions below. Use a straight piece of narrow lumber to connect your pencil marks to draw a long straight line. The string compass is explained in greater detail on page 119.

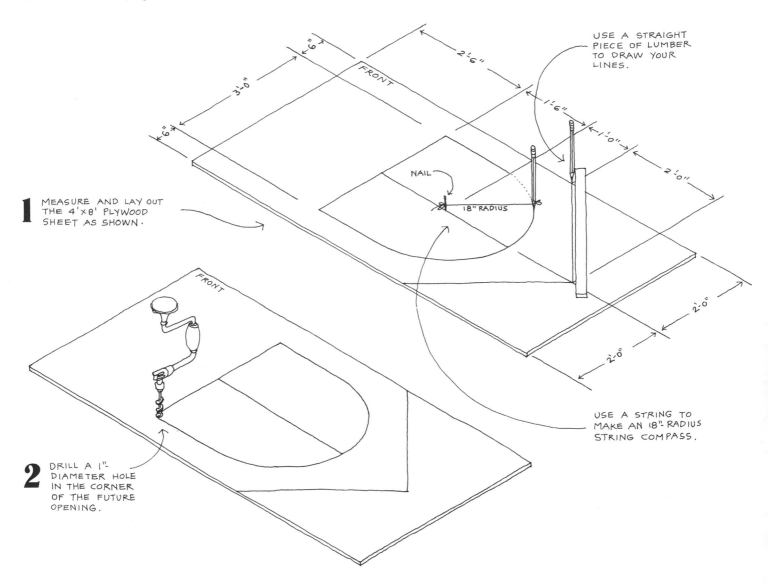

USE A STRAIGHT PIECE OF LUMBER TO DRAW YOUR LINES.

6"

3'-0"

6"

FRONT

2'-6"

1'-6"

1'-0"

2'-0"

NAIL

18" RADIUS

2'-0"

2'-0"

1 MEASURE AND LAY OUT THE 4'×8' PLYWOOD SHEET AS SHOWN.

USE A STRING TO MAKE AN 18" RADIUS STRING COMPASS.

FRONT

2 DRILL A 1" DIAMETER HOLE IN THE CORNER OF THE FUTURE OPENING.

Ben and Molly laying out the lemonade stand front on the plywood sheet.

Sawing the Parts

Below are the five steps to saw all the wooden parts needed to build your lemonade stand. Have a friend or two steady the work while you saw. You'll want to make straight saw cuts so your project will fit together perfectly. It's important to sand all pieces, removing any rough edges, before you begin to assemble your lemonade stand.

4 MEASURE AND MAKE PERPENDICULAR LINES WITH THE SQUARE AND SAW THE TWO 1X10 PARTS.

SHELF

3'-10¾"

SIGN

3 MEASURE AND MAKE PERPENDICULAR LINES WITH THE SQUARE AND SAW THE THREE 1X3 PARTS.

WASTE

SIGN

1'-5"

9¼"

9¼"

6 INSERT THE KEYHOLE SAW IN THE 1" DRILLED HOLE AND CUT OUT THE FRONT OPENING.

5 USING THE CROSSCUT SAW, CUT OUT THE TOP OF THE LEMONADE STAND FRONT.

FRONT

END

END

WASTE

WASTE

END

END

7 CROSSCUT SAW DOWN THE CENTER OF THE FRONT-OPENING PIECE TO CREATE THE TWO ENDS.

Finishing the Job

In shallow water, have friends help you lift the raft top onto the floats. Slide the floats to each end of the raft top, then nail at least three 12d nails through the sides of the raft top, angled down into the floats. After you've attached the screw eye, you'll have a way to tie the raft to a tree or a post on shore.

RAFT TOP

RAFT TOP

8 LIFT THE RAFT TOP ONTO THE FLOATS. POSITION THEM UNDER EACH END OF THE RAFT TOP.

RAFT TOP

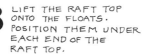

CLOCKWISE

SIDE

9 NAIL, AT AN ANGLE, THE RAFT TOP TO THE FLOATS WITH THREE 12d NAILS THROUGH EACH END OF THE SIDES.

SCREW IN THE SCREW-EYE BY TWISTING IT IN A CLOCKWISE DIRECTION WITH THE SCREWDRIVER.

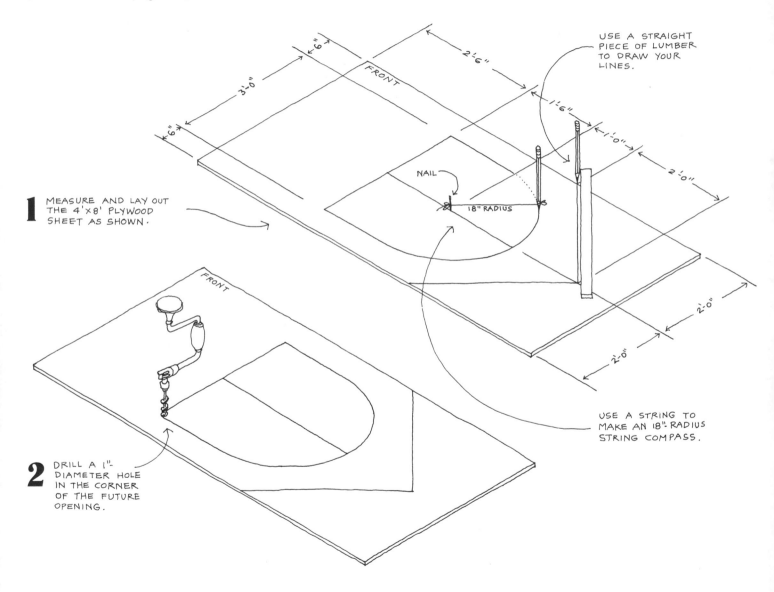

Ben keyhole-sawing the front piece.

Ben sawing the two ends, and Molly sawing the shelf.

Ben and Molly sanding all the wooden parts.

177

Making the Ends

The end pieces are designed to make a base to hold the lemonade stand in a vertical position and to support the shelf. The 1"x3" shelf supports should be nailed in place, as shown in step ten, before the rest of the lemonade stand pieces are assembled. It's much easier to do this task when the work is flat on your workbench.

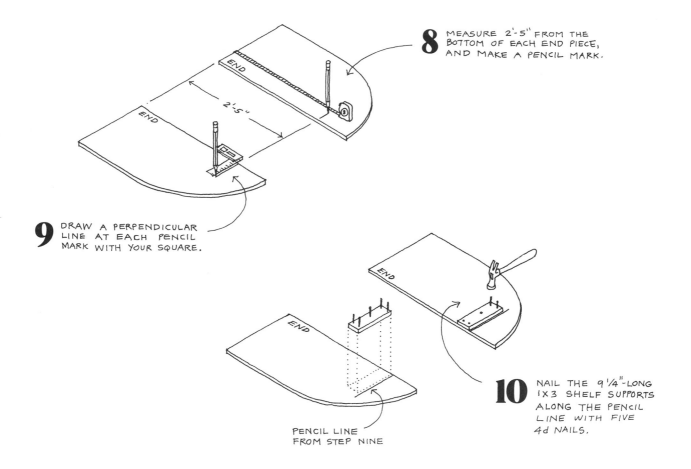

8 MEASURE 2'-5" FROM THE BOTTOM OF EACH END PIECE, AND MAKE A PENCIL MARK.

9 DRAW A PERPENDICULAR LINE AT EACH PENCIL MARK WITH YOUR SQUARE.

PENCIL LINE FROM STEP NINE

10 NAIL THE 9 1/4"-LONG 1X3 SHELF SUPPORTS ALONG THE PENCIL LINE WITH FIVE 4d NAILS.

Molly measuring and Ben nailing a shelf support to an end piece.

179

Nailing the Front to the Ends

Get a friend or two to hold the front and end pieces as you nail them together, as shown in the drawing below. To get perfect corners, make sure each end piece is lined up with the edge of the front piece before you nail. Make sure your nails are straight. If one goes in crooked, pull it out and start another one in a different place.

11 WITH SEVEN EQUALLY SPACED 8d FINISHING NAILS, NAIL THE FRONT TO EACH END PIECE.

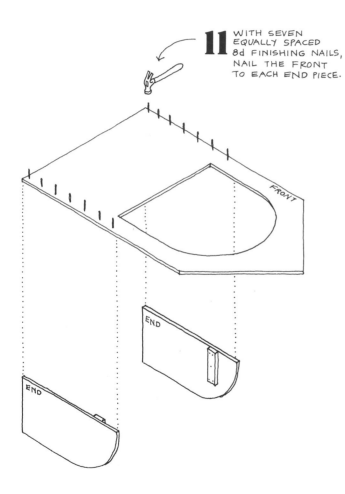

FRONT

END

END

Molly nailing as Ben steadies the work.

Finishing the Nailing

With a friend, lift the lemonade stand into its upright position and nail the shelf into place. Check to see that all rough edges are sanded. Now you're ready to paint your lemonade stand.

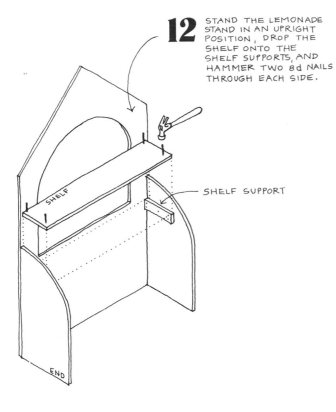

12 STAND THE LEMONADE STAND IN AN UPRIGHT POSITION, DROP THE SHELF ONTO THE SHELF SUPPORTS, AND HAMMER TWO 8d NAILS THROUGH EACH SIDE.

SHELF

END

SHELF SUPPORT

Ben and Molly lifting the shelf into place.

Painting

Using the 2" brush, carefully paint the sanded front parts of the lemonade stand with white primer paint. This'll clog the pores of the wood and provide a smooth, bright surface on which to paint the finish coat of yellow enamel. Use the ¼" signpainter's brush to make your signs after you have sketched them on the wood with a pencil. Take care and try to make perfect letters so they can be easily understood.

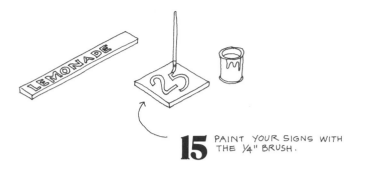

15 PAINT YOUR SIGNS WITH THE ¼" BRUSH.

13 PAINT THE FRONT AND END PIECES WITH ONE COAT OF WHITE PRIMER PAINT. LEAVE THE SHELF AND UNDERSIDE OF THE LEMONADE STAND NATURAL (UNPAINTED).

14 WHEN THE PRIMER PAINT HAS DRIED, SAND LIGHTLY, CLEAN, AND PAINT WITH ONE THICK COAT OF YELLOW ENAMEL. ALLOW IT TO DRY OVERNIGHT.

LEVEL THE LEMONADE STAND WITH AN ORANGE CRATE SO THE PAINT WILL NOT RUN.

Ben and Adam painting the final coat on the lemonade stand. Jess and Molly finishing the signs.

Setting Up for Business

After you've nailed your signs to the lemonade stand (with 4d nails), you're ready to set up your business. Near your home, find a place busy with people and arrange your lemonade stand so that it'll be seen by the most people. You'll have to buy the lemonade ingredients and paper cups and borrow a big pitcher or thermos container. You'll also need ice. If it's a hot day, you'll be surprised at how fast you sell out, so be prepared to get more ingredients quickly.

The lemonade stand is also good for selling fruit and vegetables that can be eaten on the spot, like peaches, apples, and bananas. Good luck with your new business.

Ben finishing the signs, while Molly sells lemonade to Jess and Adam.

Coaster Car

The coaster car is designed to coast down hills and give you the sensation of driving a racing car. It's the most difficult project in the book and will provide a real test for your carpentry abilities. If you can build this car without much adult supervision, someday you may want to become a carpenter because you've got the ability.

The coaster car has moving parts and will be used in relatively dangerous situations, so your work must be of high quality. If your nails are not straight and your sawing not true, your car may be weak and not function properly.

This project is quite demanding and building at least one of the one-day projects and one of the weekend projects from this book is recommended before you begin.

Assembling the Tools and Materials

Below is a list of tools and materials needed to build your coaster car. Read page 198 before you buy your wheels, and make sure the lag screws fit perfectly, as they serve as axles through the wheel holes. Hold the lag screw and spin the wheel on it to make sure it rotates smoothly and doesn't wobble. The wheels we used had a 7/16" hole, so the 7/16" lag screws were perfect as axles. Keep all your wood materials covered to prevent them from warping.

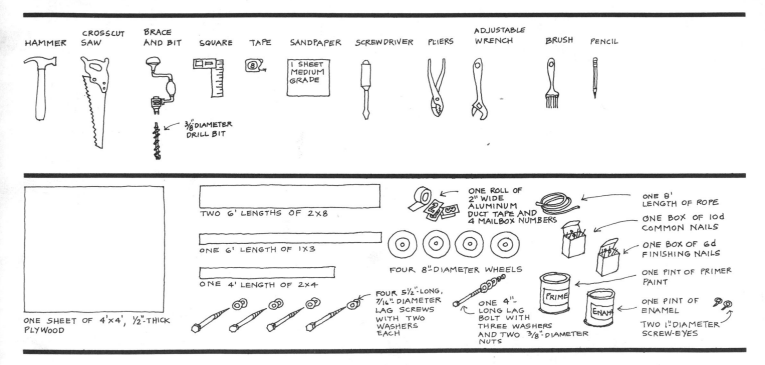

HAMMER CROSSCUT SAW BRACE AND BIT SQUARE TAPE SANDPAPER SCREWDRIVER PLIERS ADJUSTABLE WRENCH BRUSH PENCIL

1 SHEET MEDIUM GRADE

3/8" DIAMETER DRILL BIT

ONE SHEET OF 4'x4', 1/2"-THICK PLYWOOD

TWO 6' LENGTHS OF 2x8

ONE 6' LENGTH OF 1x3

ONE 4' LENGTH OF 2x4

FOUR 5½"-LONG, 7/16"-DIAMETER LAG SCREWS WITH TWO WASHERS EACH

ONE 4"-LONG LAG BOLT WITH THREE WASHERS AND TWO 3/8"-DIAMETER NUTS

ONE ROLL OF 2" WIDE ALUMINUM DUCT TAPE AND 4 MAILBOX NUMBERS

FOUR 8"-DIAMETER WHEELS

PRIME

ENAMEL

ONE 8' LENGTH OF ROPE

ONE BOX OF 10d COMMON NAILS

ONE BOX OF 6d FINISHING NAILS

ONE PINT OF PRIMER PAINT

ONE PINT OF ENAMEL

TWO 1"-DIAMETER SCREW-EYES

Jess and Molly readying the tools, while Adam and Ben unload the materials.

Laying Out the Plywood

Lay out the 4'x4' plywood sheet according to the directions below by measuring, making pencil marks, and connecting the marks with a pencil line using the 1x3 piece of lumber as a guide. Make heavy, dark pencil lines that can be clearly seen when sawing.

4½"

7⅛"

7⅛"

FRONT TOP

48"

REAR SIDE

6"

REAR SIDE

8"

REAR TOP

5⁄8"

1"

5⁄8"

20"

SEAT BACK

FRONT SIDE

21"

8½"

18"

FRONT SIDE

14½"

FRONT SIDE

21"

6"

1 MEASURE AND LAY OUT THE 4'X4' PLYWOOD SHEET AS SHOWN.

USE THE EDGE OF THE 5' LONG 1X3 TO DRAW YOUR LINES.

THE PLYWOOD PARTS LAID OUT ABOVE IN STEP ONE WILL MAKE THE BODY OF THE FINISHED COASTER CAR.

SEAT BACK

FRONT TOP

REAR SIDE

REAR TOP

FRONT SIDE

Molly and Ben laying out the plywood sheet, and Adam and Jess starting the base (page 192).

Sawing the Parts

Below are the three steps to saw all the wooden parts necessary to build your coaster car, except for the two 2x8s. If you can't buy two 6'-long pieces of 2x8, you may have to buy one 12' length and cut it in half.

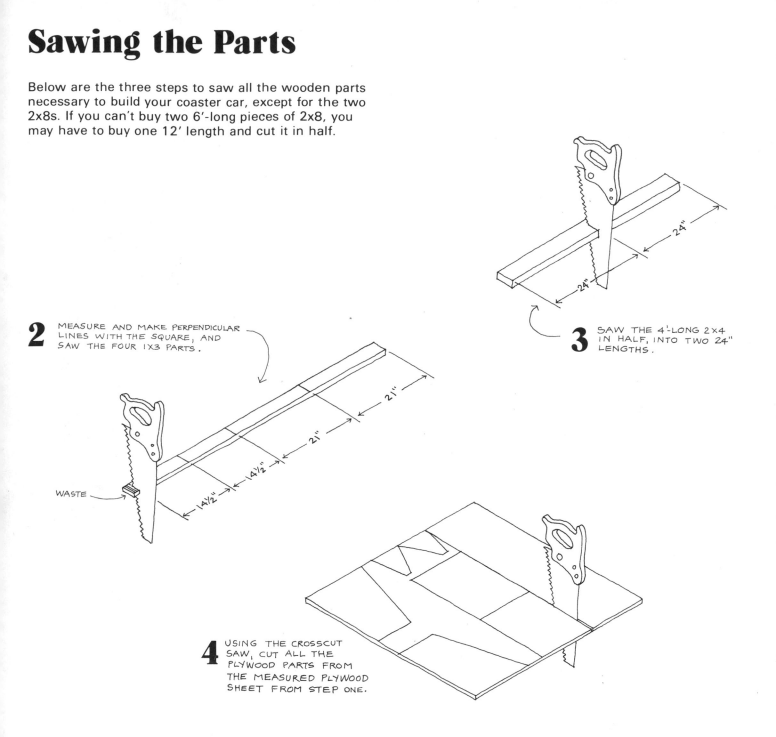

2 MEASURE AND MAKE PERPENDICULAR LINES WITH THE SQUARE, AND SAW THE FOUR 1X3 PARTS.

WASTE

21"

21"

14½"

14½"

3 SAW THE 4'-LONG 2x4 IN HALF, INTO TWO 24" LENGTHS.

24"

24"

4 USING THE CROSSCUT SAW, CUT ALL THE PLYWOOD PARTS FROM THE MEASURED PLYWOOD SHEET FROM STEP ONE.

Molly and Ben sawing the plywood sheet, while Jess and Adam cut the 1x3.

Building the Car Frame

Follow the three steps below to build your car frame. Make sure to get the 1x3s nailed perfectly in place because they'll be used to nail the plywood body parts to the car. Remember to sand all the wooden pieces before you nail them together.

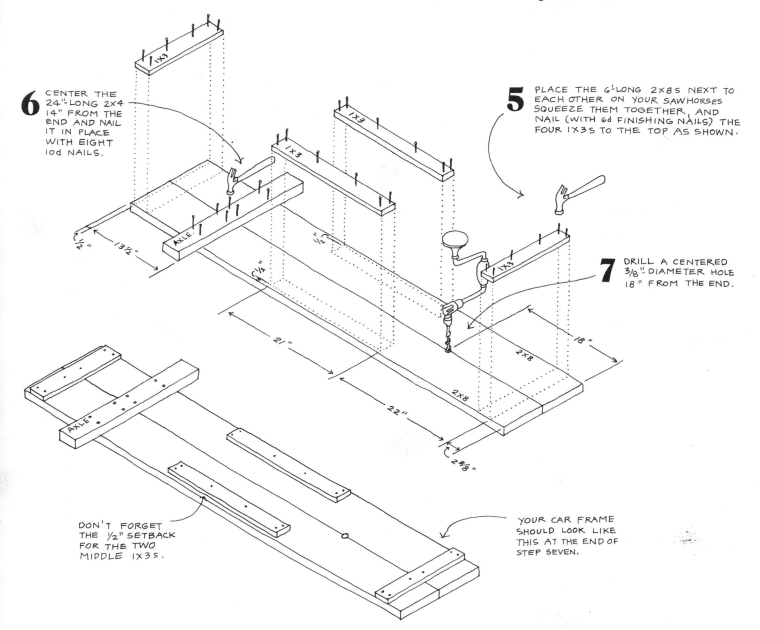

6 CENTER THE 24" LONG 2x4 14" FROM THE END AND NAIL IT IN PLACE WITH EIGHT 10d NAILS.

5 PLACE THE 6' LONG 2x8s NEXT TO EACH OTHER ON YOUR SAWHORSES SQUEEZE THEM TOGETHER, AND NAIL (WITH 6d FINISHING NAILS) THE FOUR 1x3s TO THE TOP AS SHOWN.

7 DRILL A CENTERED 3/8" DIAMETER HOLE 18" FROM THE END.

1x3

AXLE

1/2"

13 1/2"

1/2"

1/2"

21"

22"

2 3/8"

18"

2x8

2x8

1x3

AXLE

DON'T FORGET THE 1/2" SETBACK FOR THE TWO MIDDLE 1x3s.

YOUR CAR FRAME SHOULD LOOK LIKE THIS AT THE END OF STEP SEVEN.

Jess drilling the ⅜"-diameter hole. Ben and Molly nailing the rear axle to the frame.

Drilling the Wheel Holes

Drilling the holes for the wheels is the most difficult task of the coaster car project. You'll need to exert all your force against the drill, and you'll need a friend to help you hold the frame steady and put pressure against the direction you are drilling (see the photograph on the facing page).

The drilling work is very tiring. To save energy, you should change positions with your friend every few minutes, as each hole gets drilled. Take care to make sure your holes go into the wooden axles straight and true. Have your friend align the drill so that it's always straight as you work. Remember, you're drilling holes that'll receive the big screws that hold the wheels. You should try very hard to do your best work.

8 DRILL A 3/8"-DIAMETER HOLE IN THE CENTER OF THE FRONT AXLE.

FRONT AXLE

12"

12"

10 DRILL A 3/8"-DIAMETER HOLE, ABOUT 2 3/4" DEEP, INTO THE CENTER OF BOTH ENDS OF EACH AXLE.

REAR AXLE

FRONT AXLE

9 ATTACH THE FRONT AXLE TO THE FRAME BY PUSHING THE 4" LAG BOLT THROUGH A WASHER, THEN, FROM THE BOTTOM, THROUGH THE 3/8"-DIAMETER HOLE IN THE FRAME. OVER THIS BOLT, PLACE ANOTHER WASHER, THEN THE FRONT AXLE, THEN ANOTHER WASHER, THEN THE TWO NUTS. USING THE ADJUSTABLE WRENCH, TIGHTEN THE FIRST NUT UNTIL IT SQUEEZES THE AXLE BUT STILL ALLOWS THE AXLE TO ROTATE. THEN TIGHTEN THE SECOND NUT TO THE FIRST NUT BY GRIPPING THE FIRST NUT WITH THE ADJUSTABLE WRENCH AND THE SECOND NUT WITH THE PLIERS.

Adam drilling the wheel holes while Jess puts pressure in the opposite direction.

Building the Car Body

Building the body of your coaster car is really fun because the work goes quickly, and, at last, your project starts to look like a car. Be very careful with nailing. Make sure the edges are lined up before you nail, and make sure each nail goes straight. Have a friend help you steady the plywood pieces as you work.

11 BUILD THE REAR PART OF THE CAR BODY BY NAILING THE SEAT BACK AND REAR TOP PIECES BETWEEN THE TWO REAR SIDE PIECES WITH 6d FINISHING NAILS.

REAR SIDE

REAR TOP

SEAT BACK

REAR SIDE-PIECE

14 NAIL THE REAR PART (BUILT IN STEP ELEVEN) TO THE REAR AXLE AND THE REAR 1X3 WITH 6d FINISHING NAILS.

SEAT BACK

FRONT TOP

13 NAIL THE FRONT TOP TO THE FRONT SIDES AND THE FRONT 1X3 WITH 6d FINISHING NAILS.

REAR 1X3

REAR AXLE

FRONT SIDE

FRONT SIDE

1X3

FRONT AXLE

FRONT 1X3

12 NAIL THE TWO FRONT SIDES TO THE 1X3s WITH 6d FINISHING NAILS.

Ben and Molly nailing the front side pieces into place.

Jess and Molly building the rear part.

Ben nailing the front top piece into place.

Adam and Molly nailing the rear part into place.

197

Installing the Wheels

Our wheels were purchased from MTD Products Incorporated, Cleveland, Ohio 44111 through our local hardware store (order four 8x175 wheel assemblies, catalog number 734-538), but if you can find a set from a discarded baby carriage or laundry cart, you may be better off. They are easier to install and are smoother, and faster than the MTD Products' wheels. Instructions for attaching both kinds of wheels to the coaster car are shown below.

You'll need all your strength to screw the lag screws into their holes. Have patience and take a few breaks.

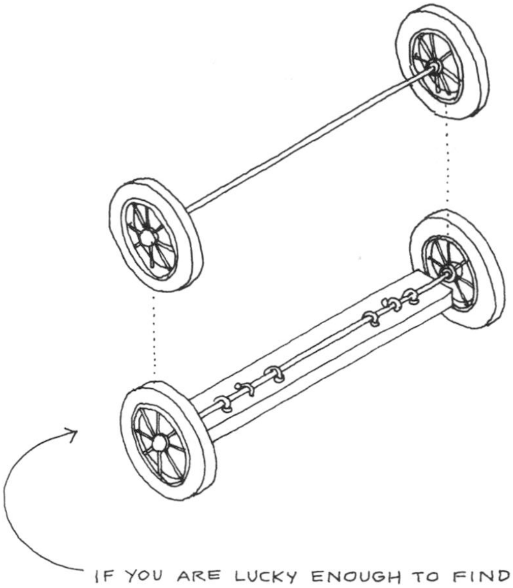

IF YOU ARE LUCKY ENOUGH TO FIND A SET OF WHEELS FROM A BABY CARRIAGE OR LAUNDRY CART (THEY ARE ALWAYS ATTACHED TO AN AXLE), YOU CAN SKIP STEP FIFTEEN AND ATTACH THESE WHEELS TO THE WOODEN AXLES BY BENDING A FEW 10d COMMON NAILS OVER THEM.

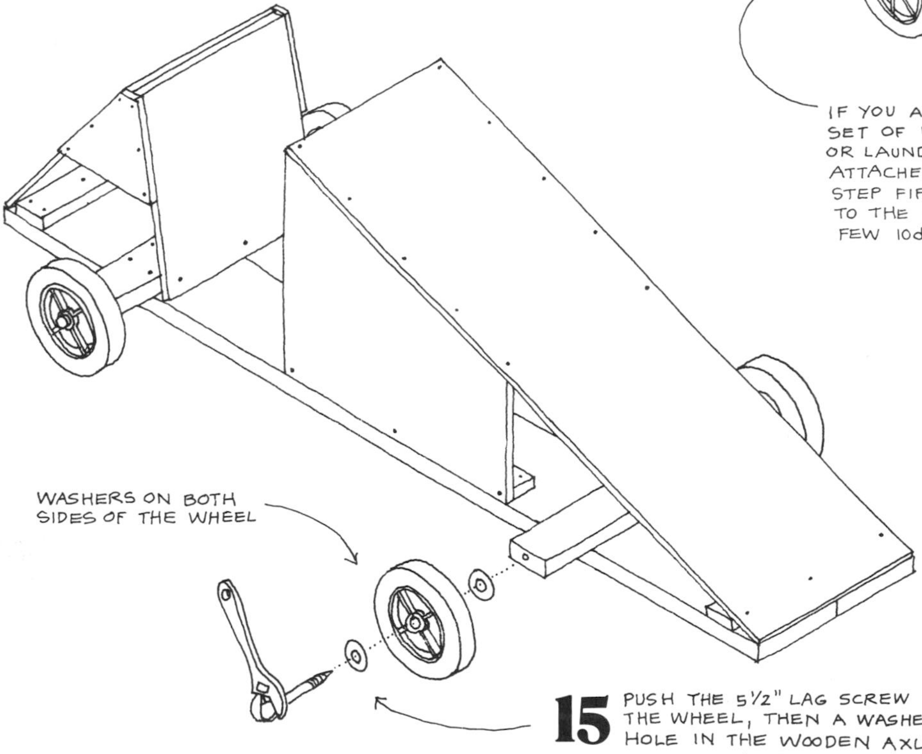

WASHERS ON BOTH SIDES OF THE WHEEL

15 PUSH THE 5½" LAG SCREW THROUGH A WASHER, THEN THE WHEEL, THEN A WASHER, THEN INTO THE DRILLED HOLE IN THE WOODEN AXLE. HAMMER THE SCREW INTO THE HOLE ABOUT ½", THEN, USING THE ADJUSTABLE WRENCH, TURN THE SCREW IN A CLOCKWISE DIRECTION UNTIL IT IS INTO THE HOLE AS FAR AS IT WILL GO AND STILL ALLOW THE WHEEL TO SPIN. DO THIS TO ALL FOUR WHEELS.

Molly starting a wheel, while Adam finishes screwing in a front wheel with the adjustable wrench.

Attaching the Steering Rope

Use the screwdriver to twist the 1"-diameter screw-eyes into each side of the front axle. After tying each end of the rope to the screw eyes, your steering rope is complete. Make sure the screw-eyes are tight and the rope knots are strong before test driving.

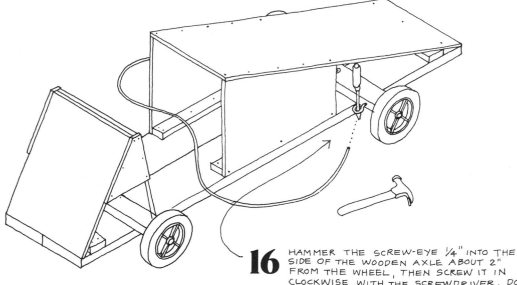

16 HAMMER THE SCREW-EYE ¼" INTO THE SIDE OF THE WOODEN AXLE ABOUT 2" FROM THE WHEEL, THEN SCREW IT IN CLOCKWISE WITH THE SCREWDRIVER. DO THIS WITH ANOTHER SCREW-EYE ON THE OTHER SIDE OF THE FRONT AXLE. TIE EACH END OF THE ROPE TO THE SCREW-EYES.

Jess tying the steering rope to a screw eye.

Painting

Using the 2" brush, carefully paint the outside of the sanded plywood parts of the coaster car with white primer paint. This will give you a clean, bright surface on which to paint your finish coat of enamel. Be careful as you paint — you'll want your car to look like a professional racing machine.

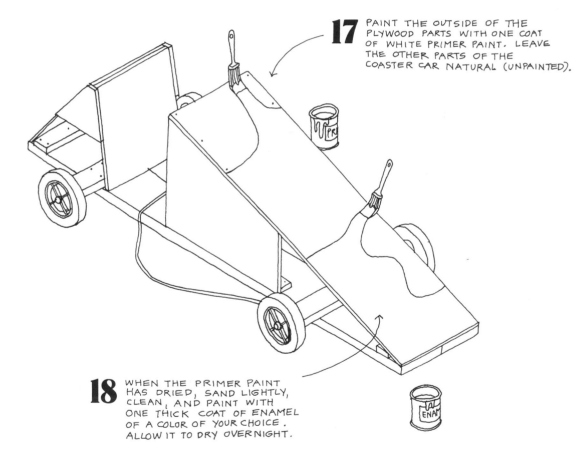

17 PAINT THE OUTSIDE OF THE PLYWOOD PARTS WITH ONE COAT OF WHITE PRIMER PAINT. LEAVE THE OTHER PARTS OF THE COASTER CAR NATURAL (UNPAINTED).

18 WHEN THE PRIMER PAINT HAS DRIED, SAND LIGHTLY, CLEAN, AND PAINT WITH ONE THICK COAT OF ENAMEL OF A COLOR OF YOUR CHOICE. ALLOW IT TO DRY OVERNIGHT.

Jess painting the car with primer paint *and finishing it with a coat of bright orange enamel.*

Attaching the Racing Stripes

If you like the racing car image, you'll want to follow the instructions below for finishing your coaster car. You'll need a 10' long, 2" wide roll of pressure sensitive aluminum duct tape, two pairs of pressure sensitive mailbox numbers, and, of course, your thumb to press them onto your car. These are the finishing touches, so take your time and make your coaster car look like a professional job.

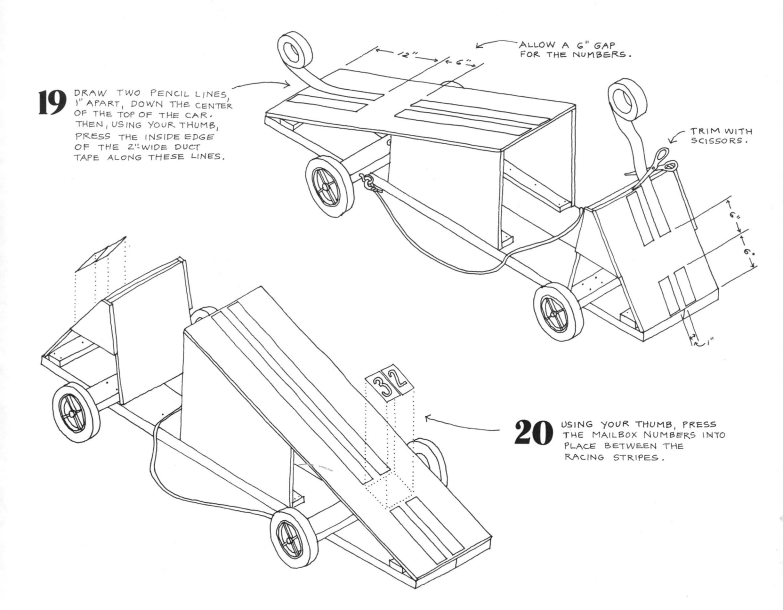

19 DRAW TWO PENCIL LINES, 1" APART, DOWN THE CENTER OF THE TOP OF THE CAR. THEN, USING YOUR THUMB, PRESS THE INSIDE EDGE OF THE 2" WIDE DUCT TAPE ALONG THESE LINES.

ALLOW A 6" GAP FOR THE NUMBERS.

12"   6"

TRIM WITH SCISSORS.

6"
6"
1"

20 USING YOUR THUMB, PRESS THE MAILBOX NUMBERS INTO PLACE BETWEEN THE RACING STRIPES.

32

Jess finishing the last racing stripe.

Test Driving

Test driving your coaster car is very, very important. You must find out if it functions well, and you must get used to driving it. Start out on a gentle, paved slope and work your way up to a steeper grade. This car is designed for one person, so take care not to abuse it — you'll want your car to last.

Remember, coaster cars have *no brakes,* so you must choose a safe place to drive, and you must learn how to drive well. Good luck, and be careful.

Jess test driving the coaster car, with help from Adam and Molly.